learning
LATEX

learning
LATEX

David F. Griffiths
University of Dundee
Dundee, Scotland

Desmond J. Higham
University of Strathclyde
Glasgow, Scotland

Society for Industrial and Applied Mathematics
Philadelphia

Library of Congress Cataloging-in-Publication Data

Griffiths, D. F. (David Francis)
   Learning LATEX / David F. Griffiths, Desmond J. Higham.
      p. cm.
   Includes bibliographical references and index.
   ISBN 978-0-898713-83-1 (pbk.)
   1. LaTeX (Computer file) 2. Computerized typesetting.
 3. Mathematics printing--Data processing. I. Higham, D. J.
   (Desmond J.) II. Title.
   Z253.4.L38G75 1996
   686.2'2544536--dc20   96-43340

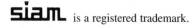

To Anne and Catherine

Contents

Preface

In this book you will find a brief introduction to the LaTeX system for typesetting documents. LaTeX, usually pronounced "lay-teck", is widely used throughout the sciences and is available, free of charge, for almost any computer. We describe version LaTeX 2_ε, usually pronounced "lay-teck two-ee", which has superseded the older version, commonly referred to as LaTeX 2.09.

Because of its popularity, every year a new batch of students and researchers want to pick up the rudiments of LaTeX. Although many books about LaTeX have been written, we feel that there is a niche for a short, lively introduction that covers the essential material while avoiding unnecessary detail. (In practice, most LaTeX users get by with a small vocabulary of commands.)

This book is aimed squarely at LaTeX beginners who wish to learn the basics with a minimum of fuss. We see our target audience falling into two main groups: students faced with the prospect of producing a report or thesis for the first time, and more experienced users of older typesetting systems like `troff` who have long planned to learn LaTeX. Various incarnations of this book have been used in undergraduate and postgraduate classes at the University of Dundee, and we have found the treatment to be suitable for a short course on mathematical typesetting with LaTeX (typically two hours of lectures and three hours of supervised computer laboratories).

We firmly believe that the best way to teach LaTeX is by example. Hence, a large part of the book consists of "before and after" illustrations showing the effect of LaTeX commands.

The book is organized as follows. Chapter 1 lists possible motivations for learning LaTeX, introduces the key high-level concepts, and points to other resources that are available.

Chapter 2 deals with common low-level formatting commands and Chapter 3 covers mathematical typesetting. Essential high-level commands are introduced in Chapter 4, which also gives tips on troubleshooting. In Chapter 5, more advanced issues are treated, including the use of packages.

Appendix A outlines how LaTeX's current version, LaTeX 2_ε, differs from the older version, LaTeX 2.09. Examples of complete LaTeX documents are provided in Appendix B and Appendix C, and the production of slides is treated in Appendix D. Finally, Appendix E lists some LaTeX-related Internet sites.

This book was prepared when both authors were at the University of Dundee. We thank the UNIX administrators Nick Dawes, Colin Macleod, and Brian Russell for their technical support. David Carlisle, Penny Davies, and Larry Shampine commented on an almost-final version of the book, and numerous students provided feedback on the material. Nick Higham gave expert advice on many of the issues that we faced and scrutinized several versions of the manuscript (on the implicit understanding that we would refer to [4]).

Finally, we acknowledge the efforts of all those who have helped to make LaTeX such a valuable tool for the scientific community, especially Donald Knuth [5], Leslie Lamport [6], and the team members involved in the LaTeX3 Project.

David F. Griffiths
Desmond J. Higham

Chapter 1

Preamble

1.1 Should You Be Reading This Book?

Most readers of this book will have already heard something about LaTeX. Perhaps a friend or colleague recommended it to you, or maybe your professor advised you to learn about it. LaTeX is a computer typesetting system that specializes in producing mathematically oriented documents. It provides transparent access to the time-honored craft of mathematical typesetting and can be used to produce a range of documents, including class handouts, reports, letters, overhead transparencies, theses, journal articles, and books.

We have written this book for LaTeX beginners and have strived to present a palatable and readable introduction with a minimum of fuss and detail. The only prerequisite is a certain amount of computing experience. You should know how to produce ASCII files with an editor, and you should have the LaTeX package available. (Information about where to obtain LaTeX software over the Internet can be found on page 70.) To appreciate the basic idea of controlling the output with a sequence of commands, knowledge of at least one programming language would be helpful.

In the interest of brevity and clarity, some of the things we say about LaTeX are slightly incomplete and a vast amount is left unsaid. We hope that this book will build your expertise to the extent that, on those occasions when you need to know more, you feel confident enough to consult one of the comprehensive references (see §1.4).

We describe the current version of LaTeX, that is, LaTeX 2_ε. In Appendix A we discuss how this differs from the older version, LaTeX 2.09.

1.2 Motivation

There are several good reasons for learning LaTeX.

- Mathematical formulas can be produced quite easily. TeX [5], the program underneath LaTeX, incorporates a great deal of knowledge about

1

formatting mathematics and hence your documents will look polished.

- Equations, citations, figures, tables, etc. can be labeled, so that cross-referencing is automated.

- LATEX is installed at many universities and research institutions and can be run on PCs, workstations, and mainframe computers. The program, plus many add-on enhancements written by enthusiasts throughout the world, is freely available over the Internet.

- The `tex` files have the standard ASCII format, and hence they can be produced using your favorite text editor and e-mailed to your friends and colleagues.

- The `dvi` files produced by the system can be sent to a variety of output devices, including the computer screen and virtually all types of printers.

- LATEX skills are useful if you are pursuing an academic career. Many journals now encourage authors to submit manuscripts electronically using LATEX (or similar systems such as TEX and AMS-TEX).

LATEX is not a WYSIWYG (What You See Is What You Get) system. Hence it lacks the obvious attraction of a real-time display of the formatted output. However, the alternative *logical design* approach of LATEX offers advantages for most scientific authors. Scientific documents contain structures such as sections, subsections, computer program listings, theorems, and mathematical variables. LATEX forces you to think in terms of these structures, rather than concentrating on the appearance of the final product. In other words, your creative efforts are focused on content rather than style. After creating the document, you can completely alter its appearance by changing a small number of formatting commands. For example, it is a simple matter to change the size of the typeface or to move from one to two columns per page.

A word of warning is in order. LATEX makes it possible to produce an impressive-looking document that is riddled with mistakes and inconsistencies. Hence, you should not be deceived by the æsthetics of the output. When you write a scientific document, your main concern should be to present your ideas clearly and correctly. LATEX has been designed to relieve you of the burden of typesetting so that you can concentrate on the substance. If you wish to learn more about *writing* in the mathematical sciences then we recommend [4], which covers a range of topics, including choosing notation, formatting equations, English usage, punctuation, revising a draft, writing slides for a talk, and publishing a paper. It also discusses computing aids such as filters, pipes, and spellcheckers.

1.3 Running LATEX

The precise details of how to run LATEX depend upon the type of computer that you are using. Your local system administrator (or, if you installed the program yourself, the accompanying documentation) should tell you what commands to use. However, the general approach is common to all versions—you must create a file with a **tex** extension, let us call it **first.tex**. This file contains the text of your document, interspersed with commands that tell LATEX how it is to be formatted. The contents of the file **first.tex** do not depend on your computer system—the same file is valid for all systems. On most systems, the command to run LATEX on **first.tex** is

```
latex first.tex
```

and this produces the file **first.dvi**. The extension **dvi** stands for *device independent*. This file can be understood by any one of several output devices, in particular it can be displayed on screen or sent to a printer. In addition to **first.dvi**, files with extensions **aux** and **log** are created. (Other files with extensions such as **toc**, **idx**, and **bbl**, may also be generated.)

There are two general points to note. First, to save paper and money, you should always check that the output is correct before printing by displaying it on the screen. This is called *previewing*. Second, the **dvi** file (and the corresponding **ps** file if you have converted from **dvi** to PostScript®) can be very large, taking up a lot of disk space. Hence, it is good practice to delete such files (but not, of course, your **tex** file) as soon as you have made use of them—they can be regenerated from the **tex** files if necessary.

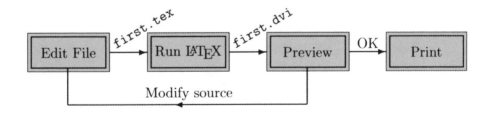

Figure 1.1: The usual sequence of commands for generating a LATEX document.

1.4 Resources

The authoritative LATEX references are [3, 6]. Lamport's book [6] is a comprehensive manual; the first few chapters give a detailed, but relatively gentle, introduction and the latter part constitutes a complete technical specification. The encyclopedic [3] is packed with information about LaTeX and the many packages that are available for its customization and extension. Anyone who uses LaTeX regularly should have access to [3] or [6].

Many other guides to LaTeX have been written. To date, only a small fraction of these apply to the current version, LaTeX 2_ε, although this will undoubtedly change in the future. It is our belief that, after mastering the fundamentals of LaTeX outlined in this book, the interested reader will be sufficiently well equipped to pass directly to [3] or [6], without the use of any "intermediate" guides.

By far the most valuable resource is a friend, colleague, or teacher who is skilled in LaTeX. Seeking advice from fellow humans and studying chunks of relevant LaTeX will help greatly in your ascent of the learning curve.

A third source of information is the Internet. Some details of what is available and how it may be accessed are given in Appendix E.

Chapter 2

Basic LATEX

2.1   Sample Document and Key Concepts

We begin with an example. Illustrated on the next page is a LATEX document generated from the source file `example.tex`. The contents of the file are reproduced on the left and the box on the right shows the output produced when the file is run through LATEX and displayed. We follow this convention throughout the book: raw LATEX on the left, output on the right. Of course, rather than appearing in a little box, your output will be formatted in full-size pages.

If you glance through the raw LATEX on the left of the next page (and at this stage you shouldn't look too carefully at the details) you will see various extra words preceded by the "backslash" character "\" such as `\begin{equation}` and `\end{equation}`, and special characters like $, ^, and _. These tell LATEX how to format the document. LATEX knows a large number of formatting commands, but we hope to make it clear in this book that most situations can be handled with a relatively small subset.

You will also notice the lines

`\documentclass{article}`

`\begin{document}`

at the beginning of the file and

`\end{document}`

at the end. Lines like these must appear in every LATEX document; their use is discussed in §4.1. The rest of the examples in the book are to be regarded as small chunks of LATEX that live inside a complete document, and hence they will not include these commands. Extra commands are sometimes placed between `\documentclass` and `\begin{document}`; this part of the document is known as the *preamble* (see Figure 4.1, page 37).

```
\documentclass{article}

\begin{document}

This is a short document
to illustrate the basic use of
\LaTeX.

Simply leave a blank line to
get a new paragraph;
indentation is automatic.

Mathematical expressions
such as $y = 3 \sin x$
are obtained with dollar signs.
Equations can be displayed,
as in
\[
   y = 3 \sin x.
\]
Numbered equations are also
possible:
\begin{equation}\label{equa}
   y = 3 \sin x.
\end{equation}
Because we have labeled this
equation we can refer to it
without having to know its
number.  Thus, the preceding
equation was
number~(\ref{equa}).

Powers (superscripts), as in $x^2$,
are obtained with \verb"^";
more complicated powers must live
in curly braces: $x^{2+\alpha}$.

Likewise, subscripts are obtained
with the underscore: $y_3$ or
$y_{n+1}$.

We can get both with
$x_{n+1}^{2+\alpha}$.

\end{document}
```

This is a short document to illustrate the basic use of LaTeX.

Simply leave a blank line to get a new paragraph; indentation is automatic.

Mathematical expressions such as $y = 3\sin x$ are obtained with dollar signs. Equations can be displayed, as in
$$y = 3\sin x.$$
Numbered equations are also possible:
$$y = 3\sin x. \qquad (2.1)$$
Because we have labeled this equation we can refer to it without having to know its number. Thus, the preceding equation was number (2.1).

Powers (superscripts), as in x^2, are obtained with ^; more complicated powers must live in curly braces: $x^{2+\alpha}$.

Likewise, subscripts are obtained with the underscore: y_3 or y_{n+1}.

We can get both with $x_{n+1}^{2+\alpha}$.

LATEX generally regards groups of characters separated by spaces as *words*; a "newline" generated by the Return (or Enter) key is also thought of as a space. The number of spaces between words is immaterial—the output will look the same with 1 or 20. Also, since a single "newline" character is treated as an interword space, it doesn't matter where newlines occur in the file; LATEX will make up its own mind about how to break a paragraph into lines, hyphenating words if necessary to produce neat output.

A blank line—or any number of blank lines together—signifies the end of a paragraph. Judicious use of blank lines and spaces makes your tex file much easier for others to read and understand. A paragraph is automatically indented by LATEX, except when it is the first in a section. If you want to override this feature, insert the \noindent command at the start of the new paragraph.

The following characters have a special meaning in LATEX:

\   & $ %   ˜   _   {   }   #   ^

When you want one of these characters to appear in the output, most of them can be generated by preceding the character with a backslash.

```
The special characters \&, \$,
\%, \_, \{, \}, and \# may be
printed by preceding each with
a backslash. We can then put
text in \{curly braces\}.
```

The special characters &, $, %, _, {, }, and # may be printed by preceding each with a backslash. We can then put text in {curly braces}.

If a % sign is included in a line without being preceded by a backslash, the remainder of the line is ignored. This provides a mechanism for inserting comments into the LATEX file. Look at the next example carefully and compare the input with the output.

```
It is likely that 50\% of the time
you will be frustrated because you
forgot to precede the % symbol by
a backslash.
```

It is likely that 50% of the time you will be frustrated because you forgot to precede the a backslash.

The special characters (and ordinary characters, too) can also be displayed in a typewriter font using the \verb command. For example, \verb"%˜and\" produces %˜and\. The character immediately following \verb, in this case ", acts as the opening delimiter—everything will be printed out "verbatim" up to the next occurrence of that character. The text between the delimiters should not be broken across lines in the source file. For this reason \verb is suitable only for short bursts of verbatim output.

2.2   Type Style

For variation and emphasis, the style of the type can be altered. More precisely, you can control the *shape, series,* and *family* of the type. There are four shapes

```
\textup{Upright type}
\textit{Italic type}
\textsl{Slanted type}
\textsc{Small caps type}
```

> Upright type *Italic type Slanted type*
> SMALL CAPS TYPE

and two series

```
\textmd{Medium} \textbf{Boldface}
```

> Medium **Boldface**

and three families

```
\textrm{Roman} \textsf{Sans serif}
\texttt{Typewriter}
```

> Roman Sans serif Typewriter

Note that the text whose type is to be changed is enclosed in curly braces after the command. You can combine the three features, as in

```
\textsl{Don't \textbf{overuse}
          type-changing.}
\textsf{It \textit{annoys} the
            \textsc{reader}.}
\texttt{And loses \textsl{impact}.}
```

> *Don't* **overuse** *type-changing.*   It
> *annoys* the READER.   And loses
> impact.

In addition, LATEX has the \emph command that causes the enclosed text to be emphasized. So \emph{important} becomes *important.* The particular effect produced by \emph depends on the type in current use.

```
\textsc{Pile on \emph{lots}
          of subtlety.}
\textsf{Sans serif adds a little
          \emph{je ne sais rien}.}
\textsl{Nouns should \emph{never}
          be verbed.}
```

> PILE ON *lots* OF SUBTLETY.   Sans
> serif adds a little *je ne sais rien. Nouns*
> *should* never *be verbed.*

Characters of different sizes are sometimes needed for titles, headings, etc. The default size is 10 points, a point being a printing term for approximately 1/72 of an inch. To produce an entire document in a different type size, the 11pt or 12pt options can be specified with \documentclass, as discussed in §4.1. The declarations

```
\Huge \huge \LARGE \Large \large \normalsize
\small \footnotesize \scriptsize \tiny
```

can be used to change the size selectively. These declarations, and the words to which they apply, are enclosed in curly braces to limit their scope. A space separates the command from the text.

```
{\LARGE LARGE text} makes ideal
{\Large Large text} for
shortsighted people;
{\tiny tiny text} makes
ideal {\scriptsize
scriptsize text} for
longsighted people.
```

LARGE text makes ideal Large text for shortsighted people; tiny text makes ideal scriptsize text for longsighted people.

If the particular combination of shape, series, family, and size is not available on your system, LaTeX will warn you and substitute a "nearby" alternative.

2.3 Environments

Environments are portions of the document that we want LaTeX to treat differently from the main body. They are generally created by enclosing the text between the commands

\begin{*environment name*}

...

\end{*environment name*}.

In this section we discuss some common nonmathematical environments.

2.3.1 Lists

There are several list-making environments. The `itemize` version produces "bullets".

```
\begin{itemize}
  \item Every sentence should
  make sense in isolation.
  Like that one.
  \item There is a lot to be
  said for brevity.
  \item Many words can
  ostensibly be deleted.
  \item Eschew the
  highfalutin.
  \item Understatement is a
  mindblowingly effective
  weapon.
\end{itemize}
```

- Every sentence should make sense in isolation. Like that one.

- There is a lot to be said for brevity.

- Many words can ostensibly be deleted.

- Eschew the highfalutin.

- Understatement is a mindblowingly effective weapon.

Notice how each new entry is preceded by the \item command.

Numbered lists are produced with `enumerate`.

```
\begin{enumerate}
  \item Spellcheckers are not
  perfect; they can kiss may errs.
  \item Somebody once said
  that all quotes should be
  accurately attributed.
  \item The importance of
  comprehensive
  cross-referencing will be
  covered elsewhere.
\end{enumerate}
```

1. Spellcheckers are not perfect; they can kiss may errs.

2. Somebody once said that all quotes should be accurately attributed.

3. The importance of comprehensive cross-referencing will be covered elsewhere.

In the `description` environment an optional argument enclosed between square braces after the `\item` command can be used to customize the headings. The optional argument is set in a bold typeface.

```
\begin{description}
  \item[Rule 1.] Mixed
  metaphors can kill two
  birds without a paddle.
  \item[Rule 2.] Similes
  are about as much use
  as a chocolate teapot.
  \item[Rule 3.] Sporting
  analogies won't even
  get you to first base.
\end{description}
```

Rule 1. Mixed metaphors can kill two birds without a paddle.

Rule 2. Similes are about as much use as a chocolate teapot.

Rule 3. Sporting analogies won't even get you to first base.

Lists can be nested.

```
\begin{enumerate}
  \item Punctuation
  \begin{enumerate}
    \item Don't use commas, to
    separate text unnecessarily.
    \item Avoid ugly abr'v'ns.
  \end{enumerate}
  \item Spelling
  \begin{enumerate}
    \item If there's a particular
    word you can never spell,
    use a pnemonic.
    \item Take care with pluri.
  \end{enumerate}
\end{enumerate}
```

1. Punctuation

    (a) Don't use commas, to separate text unnecessarily.

    (b) Avoid ugly abr'v'ns.

2. Spelling

    (a) If there's a particular word you can never spell, use a pnemonic.

    (b) Take care with pluri.

2.3.2 Centering

The `center` environment places text in the center of the line. The `\\` command signals the end of a line.

```
\begin{center}
   {\large\textbf{Assignment 1}}\\
   Sue d'Onym\\
   MS601
\end{center}
The answers to questions ....
```

> **Assignment 1**
> Sue d'Onym
> MS601
>
> The answers to questions ....

The spacing between successive lines in this example may be changed as described on page 14; commands for the automatic construction of titles for documents are described on page 34.

2.3.3 Tables

There are two environments related to tables. The first, called `tabular`, produces the table and the second, `table`, is used to give the table a caption and a possible key for cross-referencing.

The `tabular` environment has the form

```
\begin{tabular}{format}
...
\end{tabular}
```

where the format tells LaTeX how many columns there are to be and whether they should be left justified, (`l`), centered, (`c`), or right justified, (`r`).

```
The marks for the 1996 class
are more respectable.

\begin{tabular}{lrc}
   Name & Mark & Grade \\
   \hline
   Emma Winner      & 99 & A+ \\
   Scott Passmark   & 51 & C \\
   Shirley Knott    & 5 & F
\end{tabular}

The average mark is well over 50\%.
```

> The marks for the 1996 class are more respectable.
>
> | Name | Mark | Grade |
> |---|---|---|
> | Emma Winner | 99 | A+ |
> | Scott Passmark | 51 | C |
> | Shirley Knott | 5 | F |
>
> The average mark is well over 50%.

Notice that

- the {lrc} specifies that the first column should be left justified, the second right justified, and the third centered,

- the entries across each row of the table are separated by &,

- each line except the last terminates with \\,

- a horizontal line was created by placing \hline after the \\ command,

- blank lines precede and follow the tabular environment so that the table lives in its own paragraph (otherwise the table would be formatted as part of the surrounding text),

- the table is left justified on the page.

Vertical lines can be drawn by including | at appropriate points in the format specification. In the next example we also center the table on the page.

```
\begin{center}
 \begin{tabular}{|l||r|c|}
   \hline
   Name & Mark & Grade \\
   \hline\hline
   Emma Winner     & 99 & A+\\
   Scott Passmark & 51 & C\\
   Shirley Knott   &  5 & F\\
   \hline
 \end{tabular}
\end{center}
```

Name	Mark	Grade
Emma Winner	99	A+
Scott Passmark	51	C
Shirley Knott	5	F

In order to have entries that span more than one column of a table we use \multicolumn, as in the following example.

```
\begin{tabular}{|l||r|r|}
\hline
 & \multicolumn{2}{c|}{Marks}\\
        \cline{2-3}
Name        & MS601& MS602\\
\hline\hline
Emma Winner    & 99 & 51 \\
Scott Passmark & 51 & 50\\
Shirley Knott   &  5 & 49\\
\hline
 \end{tabular}
```

Name	Marks	
	MS601	MS602
Emma Winner	99	51
Scott Passmark	51	50
Shirley Knott	5	49

The \multicolumn command has three arguments. The first specifies how many columns it should span, the second whether to left justify, right justify, or center the entry (notice the presence also of the | which ensures that the border of the surrounding box is complete), and the third contains the content. We have also introduced another command \cline{2-3} which draws the horizontal line through columns 2 to 3. For a line spanning a single column, use \cline{2-2}, for example.

Next, we place the table in the table environment and give it a caption and a key. By designating a key after the caption with \label{mytable}, we can refer to this table anywhere in the document by \ref{mytable}, at which point the table number will be automatically inserted.

```
The results given in
Table~\ref{tab:a} show the
very satisfactory performance
of the 1996 class, whose
average is over 50\%. (Note
that we have referred to the
number of the table before it
appears.)

\begin{table}
  \begin{center}
    \begin{tabular}{lrc}\hline
      Name & Mark & Grade \\
      \hline
      Emma Winner    & 99 & A+\\
      Scott Passmark & 51 & C\\
      Shirley Knott  &  5 & F\\ \hline
    \end{tabular}
    \caption{Class Mark List}\label{tab:a}
  \end{center}
\end{table}
```

The results given in Table 2.1 show the very satisfactory performance of the 1996 class, whose average is over 50%. (Note that we have referred to the number of the table before it appears.)

Name	Mark	Grade
Emma Winner	99	A+
Scott Passmark	51	C
Shirley Knott	5	F

Table 2.1: Class Mark List

The `table` environment (as well as `figure`, which we shall meet in §5.3) is a "floating environment" that is normally placed in the output document at roughly the location where it is input. Since tables and figures can be large objects, it may not be possible for LaTeX to fit them neatly onto the current page, so they are permitted to float to a more convenient location. An *optional* argument can be added to `\begin{table}`. Specifying `\begin{table}[h]` tells LaTeX that you wish the table to appear here (where it has been typed in); other options are `[t]`, for top of page, `[b]`, for bottom of page, and `[p]`, which puts the table on a separate page containing other "floating bodies". It is possible to include more than one location specifier; `\begin{table}[thb]` tells LaTeX that our preferences are t, h, and b, in that order. The factors influencing LaTeX's table locating algorithm are many and various, so your preferences may be overridden. Stricter adherence to your preferences can be signaled by the additional specifier ! so that, for example, `[!b]` (almost) insists that the table appears at the bottom of the current page. For more details, see [6, §C.9.1]. To make the caption appear above the table instead of below, place the `\caption` command immediately after the `\begin{table}` command. An illustration of this can be seen on page 41.

2.3.4   Verbatim

Verbatim is an extremely useful environment for displaying sections of computer code, raw LATEX, etc., since it prints out the text exactly as it was input and uses a (nonproportionally spaced) typewriter font. The special characters \&$%~_{}#^ lose their LATEX significance within this environment.

```
\begin{verbatim}
% pattern.m
% Shaded region is where
% ||||x|-1|-1|-|||y|-1|-1||
%                   >=1/3

h = 0.05;   % grid spacing
[x,y] = meshgrid(-4:h:4,-4:h:4);
e = ones(size(x));
Z = abs( abs( abs( abs(x) - ...
        e) - e) - abs( ...
          abs( abs(y) - e) - e) );
spy(3*Z >= e);
\end{verbatim}
```

```
% pattern.m
% Shaded region is where
% ||||x|-1|-1|-|||y|-1|-1||
%                   >=1/3

h = 0.05;   % grid spacing
[x,y] = meshgrid(-4:h:4,-4:h:4);
e = ones(size(x));
Z = abs( abs( abs( abs(x) - ...
        e) - e) - abs( ...
          abs( abs(y) - e) - e) );
spy(3*Z >= e);
```

The alternative command \verb, which is more appropriate for short bursts of verbatim output, was discussed on page 7.

2.4   Vertical and Horizontal Spacing

The vertical spacing between lines can be altered using \bigskip, \medskip, and \smallskip. Compare the example below with that on page 11.

```
\begin{center}
  {\large\textbf{Assignment 1}}
  \medskip

  Sue d'Onym
  \smallskip

  MS601
\end{center}
\bigskip
```

Assignment 1

Sue d'Onym

MS601

The answers to questions ....

```
The answers to questions ....
```

When one of these commands occurs in the middle of a paragraph, the space is added at the end of the next complete (formatted) line, which is why they have been followed by blank lines in the preceding example. The precise spacing caused by the three skip commands depends upon certain style parameters that will not be discussed in this book.

Absolute vertical spacing is achieved with \vspace. The command

`\vspace{2.2in}`

will leave a vertical space of 2.2 inches, whereas \vspace{3.5cm} gives 3.5 centimeters. The \vspace* command forces LATEX to insert the requested space when it might otherwise suppress it (for example, at the beginning of a new page). Other units of length are mm (millimeters), em (the width of the letter "M"—the widest character), ex (the height of the letter "x"), and pt for points. Negative lengths are permitted; \vspace{-0.25in} will cause the text following it to "move up" 0.25 inches. The command \fill represents an infinitely stretchable length. So, for example, \vspace{\fill} will produce a vertical gap that extends to the foot of the page (unless this \fill is competing with another infinitely stretchable \fill).

Horizontal spacing works in a similar way using the \hspace command.

```
Get out your rulers
and measure these lengths.

\vspace{0.2in}

Push right\hspace{1in}one inch.

\vspace{0.5cm}

Push right\hspace{\fill} hard.

\vspace{0.9cm}
```

Get out your rulers and measure these lengths.

Push right   one inch.

Push right   hard.

Left   Middle   Right.

```
Left\hspace{\fill} Middle
\hspace{\fill} Right.
```

Other horizontal spacing commands that are useful for mathematical expressions are discussed on page 19.

Chapter 3

Typesetting Mathematics

3.1 Examples

The file example.tex on page 6 includes some simple mathematical typesetting. You will notice that mathematical symbols appear in an italic-like font; compare the correct form x, a, produced by x, a, with the regular roman type x, a. Single dollar signs enclose an in-line mathematical expression, whereas the delimiters \[and \] are used for unnumbered, displayed equations.

Some common mathematical symbols and the commands used to produce them are given in Table 3.1. A mathematical symbol may be negated by preceding it with the \not command. Thus, $\not<, \not\subset, \not|$ produces $\not<, \not\subset, \not|$. The commands \ne, giving $\neq$, and \notin, giving $\notin$, are already provided.

Mathematical functions such as "log" and "sin" are, by convention, typeset in standard roman type. This makes expressions easier to read; compare $\sin x, \cosh y$ with $sinx, coshy$. The former used the correct $\sin x, \cosh y$ and the latter, $sin x, cosh y$. Table 3.2 shows the built-in functions available in LATEX. You may need another function, such as "diag", which is not available. In this case you can use the \mathrm command to produce roman type in a mathematical expression. For example,

$\mathrm{diag}(1,2,3,\ldots,20)$

gives $\mathrm{diag}(1, 2, 3, \ldots, 20)$. Math fonts are discussed further on pages 22 and 30.

The ellipsis "..." in the previous expression was produced using \ldots. Notice that the dots are aligned with the base of the characters. Another form, "$\cdots$", is produced by \cdots, which may only be used in math mode. This is more appropriate for use with $+, -, =$ as in $a_1 + a_2 + \cdots + a_n$. Examples of vertical and diagonal ellipses are given on page 26.

`\alpha`	α	`\beta`	β	`\gamma`	γ	`\delta`	δ
`\epsilon`	ϵ	`\varepsilon`	ε	`\zeta`	ζ	`\eta`	η
`\theta`	θ	`\vartheta`	ϑ	`\iota`	ι	`\kappa`	κ
`\lambda`	λ	`\mu`	μ	`\nu`	ν	`\xi`	ξ
`\pi`	π	`\varpi`	ϖ	`\rho`	ρ	`\varrho`	ϱ
`\sigma`	σ	`\tau`	τ	`\upsilon`	υ	`\phi`	ϕ
`\varphi`	φ	`\chi`	χ	`\psi`	ψ	`\omega`	ω
`\Gamma`	Γ	`\Delta`	Δ	`\Theta`	Θ	`\Lambda`	Λ
`\Xi`	Ξ	`\Pi`	Π	`\Sigma`	Σ	`\Upsilon`	Υ
`\Phi`	Φ	`\Psi`	Ψ	`\Omega`	Ω		
`\pm`	$\pm$	`\mp`	$\mp$	`\times`	$\times$	`\div`	$\div$
`\cap`	$\cap$	`\cup`	$\cup$	`\vee`	$\vee$	`\wedge`	$\wedge$
`\circ`	$\circ$	`\ast`	$\ast$	`\star`	$\star$	`\diamond`	$\diamond$
`\bigcirc`	$\bigcirc$	`\cdot`	$\cdot$	`\odot`	$\odot$	`\bullet`	$\bullet$
`\oplus`	$\oplus$	`\ominus`	$\ominus$	`\otimes`	$\otimes$	`\oslash`	$\oslash$
`\nabla`	∇	`|`	$\|$	`\prime`	$\prime$	`\surd`	$\surd$
`\partial`	∂	`\ell`	ℓ	`\Re`	$\Re$	`\Im`	$\Im$
`\infty`	∞	`\triangle`	$\triangle$	`\exists`	$\exists$	`\forall`	$\forall$
`\imath`	$\imath$	`\jmath`	$\jmath$	`\emptyset`	$\emptyset$	`\backslash`	$\backslash$
`\le`	$\le$	`\ll`	$\ll$	`\geq`	$\geq$	`\gg`	$\gg$
`\subset`	$\subset$	`\subseteq`	$\subseteq$	`\supset`	$\supset$	`\supseteq`	$\supseteq$
`\in`	$\in$	`\ni`	$\ni$	`\notin`	$\notin$	`\propto`	$\propto$
`\ne`	$\ne$	`\equiv`	$\equiv$	`\approx`	$\approx$	`\sim`	$\sim$
`\perp`	$\perp$	`\parallel`	$\parallel$	`\cong`	$\cong$	`\simeq`	$\simeq$
`\sum`	$\sum$	`\prod`	$\prod$	`\int`	$\int$	`\oint`	$\oint$
`\bigcap`	$\bigcap$	`\bigcup`	$\bigcup$	`\bigoplus`	$\bigoplus$	`\bigotimes`	$\bigotimes$

Table 3.1: The Greek letters and a selection of mathematical symbols. The last two rows of symbols will scale in size to fit the context.

`\arccos`	`\cos`	`\csc`	`\exp`	`\ker`	`\limsup`	`\min`	`\sinh`
`\arcsin`	`\cosh`	`\deg`	`\gcd`	`\lg`	`\ln`	`\Pr`	`\sup`
`\arctan`	`\cot`	`\det`	`\hom`	`\lim`	`\log`	`\sec`	`\tan`
`\arg`	`\coth`	`\dim`	`\inf`	`\liminf`	`\max`	`\sin`	`\tanh`

Table 3.2: Commands for typesetting mathematical functions.

`\leftarrow`	$\leftarrow$	`\longleftarrow`	$\longleftarrow$	`\downarrow`	$\downarrow$
`\Leftarrow`	$\Leftarrow$	`\Longleftarrow`	$\Longleftarrow$	`\Downarrow`	$\Downarrow$
`\rightarrow`	$\rightarrow$	`\longrightarrow`	$\longrightarrow$	`\uparrow`	$\uparrow$
`\Rightarrow`	$\Rightarrow$	`\Longrightarrow`	$\Longrightarrow$	`\Uparrow`	$\Uparrow$
`\leftrightarrow`	$\leftrightarrow$	`\longleftrightarrow`	$\longleftrightarrow$	`\updownarrow`	$\updownarrow$
`\Leftrightarrow`	$\Leftrightarrow$	`\Longleftrightarrow`	$\Longleftrightarrow$	`\Updownarrow`	$\Updownarrow$
`\nearrow`	$\nearrow$	`\rightleftharpoons`	$\rightleftharpoons$	`\searrow`	$\searrow$
`\swarrow`	$\swarrow$	`\mapsto`	$\mapsto$	`\nwarrow`	$\nwarrow$

Table 3.3: A selection of arrows.

We continue with examples involving fractions, subscripts, and super-scripts. The command \frac for formatting fractions is always followed by two expressions that are enclosed in curly braces (the numerator and denominator). Be selective when using it within matched dollar signs (see page 29).

The characters _ and ^ produce subscripts and superscripts, respectively. An expression involving more than one symbol can be used as a subscript or superscript if it is enclosed in curly braces.

```
\[
  x = \frac{1+y}{1+2z^2}
\]

\[
  x_3 + y^{n+2} = z\sqrt{b^2-4ac}
\]

\[
  S_n = a_1 + a_2 + \cdots + a_n
\]

\[
  a_n = 3 + (-1)^n, \;
          n = 1,2,\ldots,N
\]
```

$$x = \frac{1+y}{1+2z^2}$$

$$x_3 + y^{n+2} = z\sqrt{b^2 - 4ac}$$

$$S_n = a_1 + a_2 + \cdots + a_n$$

$$a_n = 3 + (-1)^n, \; n = 1, 2, \ldots, N$$

In the last equation above, the command \; adds horizontal spacing. LATEX is very good at typesetting mathematics, but occasionally, as in the \; example above, it is necessary to help with the spacing. Horizontal spacing commands available in math mode include

Negative thin: \! ‖   Thin: \, ‖   Medium: \: ‖   Thick: \; ‖

where the distance between the vertical bars indicates the amount of space created in each case. (The normal amount of space between vertical bars is ‖.) Apart from \, these can only be used math mode. As an illustration, compare the following variants.

```
$ \sqrt{2} \sin x $

$ \sqrt{2} \, \sin x $

\bigskip

$ \int \int f(x,y) dxdy $
```

$$\sqrt{2}\sin x$$
$$\sqrt{2}\,\sin x$$

$$\int\int f(x,y)dxdy$$
$$\iint f(x,y)\,dx\,dy$$

```
$ \int \!\! \int f(x,y) \,dx \, dy $
```

In the double integral example, LATEX does not automatically recognize that dx and dy are separate entities and will treat dxdy as the product of four variables unless given extra help.

Subscripts and superscripts are treated differently when they are attached to integral, summation, or product symbols or to max, min, inf, or sup.

```
\[
  S_N = \sum_{j=1}^N a_j
\]
```

$$S_N = \sum_{j=1}^{N} a_j$$

```
\[
  \int_{x=0}^\infty e^{-x^2} dx
      = \frac{\sqrt{\pi}}{2}
\]
```

$$\int_{x=0}^{\infty} e^{-x^2} dx = \frac{\sqrt{\pi}}{2}$$

```
\[
  \lim_{n\rightarrow\infty}
      (1+x/n)^n = e^x
\]
```

$$\lim_{n\rightarrow\infty} (1 + x/n)^n = e^x$$

```
\[
  \max_{1\le x\le 2}x +
      \frac{1}{x}
      = \frac{5}{2}
\]
```

$$\max_{1\le x\le 2} x + \frac{1}{x} = \frac{5}{2}$$

$$G(x) := \prod_{i=1}^{n} f_i(x)$$

```
\[
  G(x) := \prod_{i=1}^{n} f_i(x)
\]
```

Expressions like these take on a different look when used in line rather than in displayed equations.

```
\begin{enumerate}
\item $S_N = \sum_{j=1}^N a_j$
\item $\int_{x=0}^\infty e^{-x^2}
      dx = \frac{\sqrt{\pi}}{2}$
\item $\lim_{n\rightarrow\infty}
      (1+x/n)^n = e^x $
\item $\max_{1\le x\le 2}x +
      \frac{1}{x}= \frac{5}{2}$
\item $G(x) := \prod_{i=1}^{n}
                f_i(x)$
\end{enumerate}
```

1. $S_N = \sum_{j=1}^{N} a_j$

2. $\int_{x=0}^{\infty} e^{-x^2} dx = \frac{\sqrt{\pi}}{2}$

3. $\lim_{n\to\infty}(1 + x/n)^n = e^x$

4. $\max_{1\le x\le 2} x + \frac{1}{x} = \frac{5}{2}$

5. $G(x) := \prod_{i=1}^{n} f_i(x)$

These differences are explored further in §3.8.1.

Blank spaces typed into mathematical expressions have no effect—LaTeX has very firm ideas about how much space is required. You should exploit this flexibility by including spaces that make the input more readable.

3.2   Equation Environments

We have seen that a mathematical expression can be displayed by enclosing it
in \[...\]. In this case we are using the **displaymath** environment and the
expression is not numbered. In order to get a numbered expression, we must
use the **equation** environment, which is contained in

   \begin{equation} ...\end{equation}.

If we include a labeling command, as in \label{fermat}, we can refer to the
equation by its key—\ref{fermat}—rather than its number. See the example
involving \ref{equa} on page 6. Keys, whether they be for equations, tables,
figures, or sections, must be unique.   It is good practice to use keys with
a standard format to distinguish the objects that they label.   For instance,
eq:pde for an equation, fig:circ for a figure, and so on.

   In order to format sets of equations or long equations that do not fit onto
one line we need a more elaborate environment. This is provided by

   \begin{eqnarray} ...\end{eqnarray}

which is essentially a table, with precisely three columns
formatted {rcl}, that is, right justified, centered, and left justified. Entries
within a row are separated by & and all rows except the last are terminated by
\\. Each row of the array will be numbered (and may therefore be labeled) but
numbering can be turned off by including \nonumber in the row.   A complete
set of unnumbered equations is obtained with

   \begin{eqnarray*} ...\end{eqnarray*}

It is usual, but not essential, to align equations around a relational operator,
such as =, $\le$, or $\approx$.

```
\begin{eqnarray}
 y &=& x^4 + 4              \nonumber\\
   &=& (x^2+2)^2-4x^2 \nonumber\\
   &\le&(x^2+2)^2     \label{yineq}
\end{eqnarray}
\hrule
```

$$y \;=\; x^4 + 4$$
$$=\; (x^2+2)^2 - 4x^2$$
$$\le\; (x^2+2)^2 \qquad (3.1)$$

```
\begin{eqnarray*}
         x + y + z    &=& 1,  \\
 \alpha y + (\beta+1)z &=& 1/21,\\
 \alpha\beta z         &=& 1/6.
\end{eqnarray*}
\hrule
```

$$x + y + z \;=\; 1,$$
$$\alpha y + (\beta + 1)z \;=\; 1/21,$$
$$\alpha\beta z \;=\; 1/6.$$

```
\begin{eqnarray}
 e^x  &\approx& 1+x+ x^2/2!
         + x^3/3! \nonumber\\
     & & {} + x^4/4! + x^5/5!
\end{eqnarray}
```

$$e^x \;\approx\; 1 + x + x^2/2! + x^3/3!$$
$$+ x^4/4! + x^5/5! \qquad (3.2)$$

The last example above shows how a long expression can be broken across a
line. LaTeX will not do this automatically—if your expression is too long to fit

on a single line then you must use eqnarray rather than the displaymath or
equation environments. Typically, the point at which the expression is broken
must be chosen by trial and error after previewing the output. The "empty
text" created by {} before + x^4/4! is introduced so that LaTeX treats the +
as an inter-term symbol rather than a plus sign acting upon x^4/4!. (Without
the {}, there would be too little space between + and $x^4/4!$.)

3.3 Fonts, Hats, and Underlining

The range of math symbols may be extended by typesetting them in a different
font or by modifying them with hats, tildes, or underlining.

The following example illustrates some of the fonts that can be used in
math mode. The calligraphic font \mathcal is available only for uppercase
characters and \mathbf affects only *letters, numbers, and uppercase Greek
letters*; letters are set in bold roman font rather than the italic font normally
used for math symbols (this is in accordance with the usual convention for
typesetting mathematics). The command \boldmath (page 30) can be used to
obtain other bold symbols.

```
\begin{eqnarray*}
&\mathrm{A,B,C,\ldots,x,y,z.}&
\\
&\mathbf{A,B,C,\ldots,x,y,z.}&
\\
&\mathbf{\Gamma,\ldots,\Omega,}
\mathbf{\alpha,\ldots,\omega.}&
\\
&\mathsf{A,B,C,\ldots,x,y,z.}&
\\
&\mathit{A,B,C,\ldots,x,y,z.}&
\\
&\mathcal{A,B,C,\ldots,X,Y,Z.}&
\end{eqnarray*}
```

$$A, B, C, \ldots, x, y, z.$$
$$\mathbf{A, B, C, \ldots, x, y, z.}$$
$$\mathbf{\Gamma, \ldots, \Omega, \alpha, \ldots, \omega.}$$
$$\mathsf{A, B, C, \ldots, x, y, z.}$$
$$A, B, C, \ldots, x, y, z.$$
$$\mathcal{A, B, C, \ldots, X, Y, Z.}$$

The syntax of font-changing commands in math mode is similar to that for
text mode (see page 8). However, the argument is processed in math mode and
consequently spaces are ignored. For example, $\mathit{for all} x > 0$
gives *forallx* > 0. Text can be interspersed in a math expression by using
\mbox so that $\mbox{for all } x > 0$ gives for all $x > 0$ (notice the space
included after all within \mbox).

A range of hats and tildes are also provided in order to modify symbols
in math mode; these are illustrated in Table 3.4. Unlike \underline and
\overline, the wide symbols come in just two sizes and so do not necessarily
fit their arguments. For example, $\widehat{u+v+w}$ gives $u \widehat{+ v +} w$, while
$\underline{u+v+w}$ gives $\underline{u + v + w}$.

The dots should be removed from the characters i and j if symbols are to
be placed above them. The alternatives \imath, \jmath are provided for this

\hat u	$\hat{u}$	\widehat u	$\widehat{u}$	\widehat{u+v}	$\widehat{u+v}$
\tilde u	$\tilde{u}$	\widetilde u	$\widetilde{u}$	\widetilde{u+v}	$\widetilde{u+v}$
\dot u	$\dot{u}$	\underline u	$\underline{u}$	\underline{u+v}	$\underline{u+v}$
\ddot u	$\ddot{u}$	\bar u	$\bar{u}$	\overline{u+v}	$\overline{u+v}$
\vec u	$\vec{u}$	\overline{\hat u +v}	$\overline{\hat{u}+v}$	\stackrel{\triangle}{=}	$\stackrel{\triangle}{=}$

Table 3.4: Hats and underlining.

purpose and hence $\hat\imath, \tilde\jmath$ leads to $\hat{\imath}, \tilde{\jmath}$. An example involving \stackrel is given on page 30.

3.4 Braces

The curly braces { and } have a special meaning in LATEX; for example we have seen how they enclose arguments for the \frac command. In order to make curly braces appear in mathematical expressions, we precede them with a backslash: \{ ... \}. If we use \left\{ ... \right\} instead of \{ ... \} then LATEX will automatically choose braces of an appropriate size. The same auto-sizing occurs with \left[\left(\left| and \right| \right) \right] and all the delimiters shown in Table 3.5.

The appropriate use of large braces can improve both the appearance and the readability of complicated formulas.

```
\[
p(x) = 6 [ 1+(1+(\frac{1}{2}
        + \frac{1}{6}x)x)x ]
\]
```

$$p(x) = 6[1 + (1 + (\frac{1}{2} + \frac{1}{6}x)x)x]$$

```
\[
p(x) = 6 \left[ 1+\left(1+\left(
            \frac{1}{2}+
                \frac{1}{6}x
                    \right)x        \right)x
            \right]
\]
```

$$p(x) = 6\left[1 + \left(1 + \left(\frac{1}{2} + \frac{1}{6}x\right)x\right)x\right]$$

(	(	)	)	[	[	]	]
\{	{	\}	}	\langle	$\langle$	\rangle	$\rangle$
\uparrow	$\uparrow$	\downarrow	$\downarrow$	\Uparrow	$\Uparrow$	\Downarrow	$\Downarrow$
\updownarrow	$\updownarrow$	\Updownarrow	$\Updownarrow$				|	$\|$
\lfloor	$\lfloor$	\rfloor	$\rfloor$	\lceil	$\lceil$	\rceil	$\rceil$

Table 3.5: A selection of delimiters.

Each \left must be accompanied by a \right, although the type of delimiter used need not be the same.

Limits of integration may be attached to braces by using sub/superscripts, as in the next example.

```
\begin{eqnarray*}
  \int_{1/4}^{1/2}
    \frac{ dx}{x(1-x)}& = &
      \left[
        \log \left|
            \frac{x}{1-x}
          \right|
        \right]_{1/4}^{1/2}\\
              & = & \log 3.
\end{eqnarray*}
```

$$\int_{1/4}^{1/2} \frac{dx}{x(1-x)} \; = \; \left[\log \left| \frac{x}{1-x} \right| \right]_{1/4}^{1/2}$$
$$= \; \log 3.$$

It is preferable, for example, to use $1/2$ for the limits rather than \frac{1}{2}.

The square root symbol $\sqrt{\ }$, given by \sqrt{...}, also auto-sizes and accepts an optional argument in square braces; thus \sqrt{5} gives $\sqrt{5}$ and \sqrt[3]{25} gives $\sqrt[3]{25}$.

```
Prove that, for $n \ge 1$,
\[
  \frac{1}{2} < \sqrt[n]{
    \left\{
  \frac{1\cdot3\cdots(2n-1)}
   {2\cdot4\cdots2n}\right\}} < 1.
\]
```

Prove that, for $n \geq 1$,

$$\frac{1}{2} < \sqrt[n]{\left\{ \frac{1 \cdot 3 \cdots (2n-1)}{2 \cdot 4 \cdots 2n} \right\}} < 1.$$

3.5   Arrays and Matrices

To format arrays and matrices (rectangular arrays of mathematical expressions) we use the **array** environment, *which must occur within one of the mathematical environments described in §3.2.* Each row of the array must contain the same number of entries, separated by &. As with tables, all rows except the last are terminated with \\.

```
\[
  \begin{array}{llcr}
     a   & 0  & \sin (12x) & c   \\
    a+b  & 16 & \sin (2x)  & b+c \\
    a+b+c & 8 & \sin x     & a+b+c
  \end{array}
\]
```

$$\begin{array}{llcr}
a & 0 & \sin(12x) & c \\
a+b & 16 & \sin(2x) & b+c \\
a+b+c & 8 & \sin x & a+b+c
\end{array}$$

The choice {llcr} following the \begin{array} specifies that the first two columns should be left justified, the third centered and the last right justified.

An array usually forms part of a more complicated mathematical expression and is often enclosed within auto-sized braces, such as \left[and \right], described in the previous section.

```
The system may be
written in the matrix--vector
form $A \mathbf{u}
  = \mathbf{e}$, where
\[
A =
  \left[
    \begin{array}{ccc}
      1   & 1   & 1\\
      x   & y   & z\\
      x^2 & y^2 & z^2
    \end{array}
  \right], \;
\mathbf{u} =
  \left[
    \begin{array}{c}
      x \\ y \\ z
    \end{array}
  \right]
\]
```

The system may be written in the matrix–vector form $A\mathbf{u} = \mathbf{e}$, where

$$A = \begin{bmatrix} 1 & 1 & 1 \\ x & y & z \\ x^2 & y^2 & z^2 \end{bmatrix}, \quad \mathbf{u} = \begin{bmatrix} x \\ y \\ z \end{bmatrix}$$

and $\mathbf{e} = [1,1,1]^T$. The determinant of A is given by

$$\begin{vmatrix} 1 & 1 & 1 \\ x & y & z \\ x^2 & y^2 & z^2 \end{vmatrix} = (x-y)(y-z)(z-x),$$

so A is nonsingular precisely when the three values x, y, z are distinct.

```
and $\mathbf{e} = [1,1,1]^T$. The determinant of $A$ is given by
\[
\left|  \begin{array}{ccc}
    1   & 1   & 1\\
    x   & y   & z\\
    x^2 & y^2 & z^2
  \end{array} \right|  = (x-y)(y-z)(z-x),
\]
so $A$ is nonsingular precisely when the three values $x,y,z$
are distinct.
```

The following construction is useful.

```
The Kronecker delta is defined by
\[
\delta_{ij} =
  \left\{
    \begin{array}{ll}
      1 & \mbox{when $i=j$}, \\
      0 & \mbox{when $i\ne j$}.
    \end{array}
  \right.
\]
```

The Kronecker delta is defined by

$$\delta_{ij} = \begin{cases} 1 & \text{when } i = j, \\ 0 & \text{when } i \neq j. \end{cases}$$

Here, we have used \right. instead of \right\}. This creates a "dummy" right brace. (Without the dummy, LATEX would complain that \left\{ did not have a matching partner.) Generally, \left. and \right. can be used to create a dummy partner for any auto-sized delimiter. The example also makes use of the \mbox{...} command—upon entering the curly braces LATEX temporarily leaves the mathematics typesetting mode, giving the requisite roman type and the interword spacing associated with text mode.

The ellipses \ldots and \cdots mentioned on page 17, along with the vertical and diagonal versions \vdots and \ddots, are useful for formatting matrices.

```
The $N\times N$
tridiagonal matrix $T$,
defined by
\[
T = \left[
  \begin{array}{ccccc}
    a & b  & 0  &\cdots& 0\\
    c & a  & b  & &\vdots\\
    0 &\ddots&\ddots&\ddots& 0\\
    \vdots&  & c & a & b\\
    0 &\cdots & 0 & c & a
  \end{array}
  \right],
\]
has
eigenvalues
\[
    \lambda_j = a + 2\sqrt{bc}
    \cos \frac{\pi j}{N+1},\; 1 \le j \le N.
\]
```

The $N \times N$ tridiagonal matrix T, defined by

$$T = \left[\begin{array}{ccccc} a & b & 0 & \cdots & 0 \\ c & a & b & & \vdots \\ 0 & \ddots & \ddots & \ddots & 0 \\ \vdots & & c & a & b \\ 0 & \cdots & 0 & c & a \end{array} \right],$$

has eigenvalues

$$\lambda_j = a + 2\sqrt{bc}\cos\frac{\pi j}{N+1},\ 1 \le j \le N.$$

3.6 Customized Commands

LaTeX is a verbose language. Commands tend to be long strings that become tedious to type. To overcome this, we can define abbreviations using \newcommand, the syntax of which is \newcommand{*name*}{*definition*}.

```
\newcommand{\Dtn}{\Delta t_n}
Let $\Dtn := t_{n+1} - t_n$
denote the stepsize. Then the
local error is $O(\Dtn^2)$.
```

Let $\Delta t_n := t_{n+1} - t_n$ denote the stepsize. Then the local error is $O(\Delta t_n^2)$.

In this example we have defined a command \Dtn. Once it has been defined, every subsequent occurrence of \Dtn will be equivalent to \Delta t_n. Making definitions in this way offers three distinct advantages. First, it is quicker to type the shortened version. Second, it is easier to understand and debug complicated expressions if they consist of neat units. Third, if we decide to change our notation then we need only alter the definition, rather than all occurrences of the symbol.

There is a major difference between the two definitions

    \newcommand{\Dtna}{\Delta t_n}
    \newcommand{\Dtnb}{Δt_n}

The first can be used only in math mode, as in $\Dtna$. The second, however, must be used outside math mode, since, for example, `$\Dtnb$` is equivalent to `$$\Delta t_n$$`, which does not give the desired effect. This kind of difficulty can be avoided by using `\ensuremath`. If we have

```
\newcommand{\Dtn}{\ensuremath{\Delta t_n}}
```

then `\Dtn` is equivalent to `\Delta t_n` inside math mode and `$\Delta t_n$` outside math mode.

It is possible to include one or more arguments in a definition. The number of arguments (if nonzero) appears inside square braces between the name and the definition. Suppose we make the definition

```
\newcommand{\intab}[1]{\int_a^b #1 \,dx}
```

In this case there is just one argument, signified by `[1]`. The `#1` shows where in the definition the argument is to appear. When we use the definition, we enclose the required argument in curly braces:

```
\[
  \intab{x^2} = (b^3 - a^3)/3
\]
```

$$\int_a^b x^2 \, dx = (b^3 - a^3)/3$$

Here, `\intab{x^2}` is equivalent to `\int_a^b x^2 \, dx`. An example with two arguments is

```
\newcommand{\pnorm}[2]{\|\, #1 \,\|_{#2}}
```

This can be used in

```
$\pnorm{A}{2}$ denotes the
Euclidean norm.
```

$\| A \|_2$ denotes the Euclidean norm.
$\| A \|_p$, for $p \geq 1$, denotes the general p-norm.

```
$\pnorm{A}{p}$, for $p \ge 1$,
denotes the general $p$-norm.
```

It is good practice either to collect all `\newcommand` definitions together in the preamble at the start of the document or to put them in a separate file that can be read in with the `\input` command described in §5.2.

An error will result if you inadvertently set up a `\newcommand` with the name of an existing LaTeX command or one that you have already used.

3.7   Theorem-like Environments

Mathematical documents often contain structures like lemmas, theorems, assumptions, results, and so on. The `\newtheorem` command allows you to define appropriate environments—this ensures that the formatting is consistent and that the numbering and cross-referencing is automated.

For example, suppose we include the line

```
\newtheorem{thm}{Theorem}
```

(as for `\newcommands`, this is best put in the preamble or in a separate customization file). This defines an environment called `thm`, specified by the first argument, which produces structures with the heading Theorem, stipulated by the second argument.

```
\begin{thm}[Anon.]\label{means}
  Let $A = (x+y)/2$,
  $G = \sqrt{xy}$ and
  $H = 2xy/(x+y)$ denote the
  \emph{arithmetic, geometric}
  and \emph{harmonic} means
  of the two positive numbers
  $x$ and $y$. Then
  \[
    A\ge G\ge H.
  \]
\end{thm}
\noindent
\textbf{Proof} ....
```

> **Theorem 1 (Anon.)** *Let* $A = (x + y)/2$, $G = \sqrt{xy}$ *and* $H = 2xy/(x + y)$ *denote the* arithmetic, geometric *and* harmonic *means of the two positive numbers* x *and* y. *Then*
>
> $$A \geq G \geq H.$$
>
> **Proof** ....

An optional argument in square braces, such as `Anon.` in the above example, allows attribution or other remarks to be added. The key may be used for cross-referencing, as in `Theorem~\ref{means}`.

It is possible to make the numbering scheme operate relative to the section or chapter numbers, and also to make different theorem-like environments share the same numbering scheme. An example of the latter is given by the definition

```
\newtheorem{princ}[thm]{Principle}
```

in which the optional argument `thm` specifies that `princ` structures should share the same numbering scheme as `thm`. For example

```
\begin{princ} \label{keyprinc}
  The average number of
  arbitrary constants per page
  should not exceed $3.57$.
\end{princ}
```

> **Principle 2** *The average number of arbitrary constants per page should not exceed* 3.57.

Changing the optional argument `thm` to `section` would produce a heading where, for example, 7.1 signifies the first Principle of section 7. We refer the reader to [6, §3.4.3] for further details.

3.8 Math Miscellany

3.8.1 Math Styles

The examples on page 20 show that some expressions are formatted in different styles depending on whether they are part of an in-line math expression (known as *text style*) or contained in a displayed equation (known as *display style*). Also available are *script style*, which describes how sub/superscripts are formatted, and *scriptscript style* which relates to a further level of sub/superscripts.

```
In \emph{display style} we have
\[
   \sum_{j=1}^n j^2 = \frac{1}{6}
     n(n+1)(2n+1),
\]
whereas $\sum_{j=1}^n j=
\frac{1}{2}n(n+1)$
appears in \emph{text style}.
```

In *display style* we have

$$\sum_{j=1}^n j^2 = \frac{1}{6}n(n+1)(2n+1),$$

whereas $\sum_{j=1}^n j = \frac{1}{2}n(n+1)$ appears in *text style*.

You can set the formatting of a particular style with one of the declarations

\displaystyle, \textstyle, \scriptstyle, \scriptscriptstyle

as illustrated in the next example. Once one of these declarations is invoked, it remains in effect until the end of the current math mode unless it and the expression to be affected are enclosed in curly braces. These rules are similar to those that apply to \large, etc. described on page 8. (Note that \large, \Large, and the other size-changing commands apply only to text mode and cannot be used in math mode.)

```
Overriding the default
styles gives
\[
   \textstyle\sum_{j=1}^n j^2 =
      \frac{1}{6} n(n+1)(2n+1),
\]
and ${\displaystyle\sum_{j=1}^n} j
   = \frac{1}{2}n(n+1)$.
```

Overriding the default styles gives

$$\sum_{j=1}^n j^2 = \frac{1}{6}n(n+1)(2n+1),$$

and $\displaystyle\sum_{j=1}^n j = \frac{1}{2}n(n+1).$

The scope of \displaystyle in the previous example was restricted to the summation symbol.

The new command \FR{...}{...} defined in the next example makes use of \textstyle to produce fractions that are smaller than the normal size in a displayed formula.

```
\newcommand{\FR}[2]{
    {\textstyle \frac{#1}{#2}}}
\[
 u_j = \FR{3}{4}
          \sin^2 \FR{1}{2} \pi jh
\]
while
\[
 v_j = \frac{1}{4}
          \cos^2\frac{1}{2}\pi jh.
\]
```

$$u_j = \tfrac{3}{4}\sin^2 \tfrac{1}{2}\pi jh$$

while

$$v_j = \frac{1}{4}\cos^2 \frac{1}{2}\pi jh.$$

The use of \frac should generally be avoided with in-line expressions; $w = (z+1)/(z-1)$, produced with $w=(z+1)/(z-1)$, is rather more elegant than $w = \frac{z+1}{z-1}$, produced with $w=\frac{z+1}{z-1}$.

Customized commands can simplify the construction of a complex object.

```
\newcommand{\stk}[1]{\stackrel{#1}
               {\longrightarrow}}
\newcommand{\cT}{\mathcal{T}}
\newcommand{\dwn}[1]{
       {\scriptstyle #1}\downarrow}
\[
  \begin{array}{ccc}
     U          & \stk{G} & \cT U\\
   \dwn{\phi} &          & \dwn{\cT\phi}\\
   \phi(U)    & \stk{\cT\phi\circ G\circ\phi^{-1}} & \cT\phi(\cT U)
   \end{array}
\]
```

$$
\begin{array}{ccc}
U & \stackrel{G}{\longrightarrow} & \mathcal{T}U\\
{\scriptstyle\phi}\downarrow & & {\scriptstyle\mathcal{T}\phi}\downarrow\\
\phi(U) & \stackrel{\mathcal{T}\phi\circ G\circ\phi^{-1}}{\longrightarrow} & \mathcal{T}\phi(\mathcal{T}U)
\end{array}
$$

The \stackrel command stacks the first argument (in \scriptstyle) above the second argument (see Table 3.4). The customized command \dwn, which is analogous to \stk, places symbols (in \scriptstyle) alongside a downarrow.

3.8.2   Bold Math

The command \mathbf{...} introduced on page 22 can be used in math mode to obtain bold letters, numbers, and uppercase Greek letters. Other symbols, such as $=$ and $\geq$, or entire formulas, may be set in bold font with \boldmath. This is a declaration that must *not* be used in math mode. Letters are set in bold italic font. Both the commands

```
{\boldmath $a\times b = c$}
```

and

```
\boldmath $a\times b = c$ \unboldmath
```

give $\boldsymbol{a \times b = c}$, which should be compared with $\mathbf{a} \times \mathbf{b} = \mathbf{c}$ produced by

```
$\mathbf{a\times b = c}$.
```

To use \boldmath on part of a displayed equation it is necessary to leave math mode temporarily by using an \mbox, as illustrated in our next example, which produces bold symbols.

```
\newcommand{\bfa}[1]{\mathbf{#1}}
\newcommand{\bfb}[1]{
        \mbox{\boldmath $ #1 $}}
Our model is
\[
\bfa{u}\bfb{\cdot \nabla}\bfa{u}
  = \bfb{\nabla} p +
     \frac{1}{R_e}\nabla^2 \bfa{u},
\]
where $R_e$ is the Reynolds number.
```

Our model is

$$
\mathbf{u}\boldsymbol{\cdot}\boldsymbol{\nabla}\mathbf{u} = \boldsymbol{\nabla}p + \frac{1}{R_e}\boldsymbol{\nabla}^2\mathbf{u},
$$

where R_e is the Reynolds number.

3.8.3 Symbols for Number Sets

The next example defines a new command to produce a symbol for the real numbers. Notice that the `\langle`...`\rangle` delimiters are used to produce the angled brackets (see Table 3.5).

```
\newcommand{\RR}{\mathrm{I\!R\!}}

For $x,y\in\RR^n$, we define
\[
  \langle x,y \rangle =
    \sum_{j=1}^n x_j y_j.
\]
```

For $x, y \in \mathrm{I\!R}^n$, we define
$$\langle x, y \rangle = \sum_{j=1}^{n} x_j y_j.$$

A math roman (upright) font was used with negative thin space to run the letters I and R together. The amount of negative space required varies with the font. In normal math font, or in math sans serif font, the definitions

```
\newcommand{\RRn}{I\!\!R}
\newcommand{\RRs}{\mathsf{I\!R}}
```

lead to $x, y \in I\!R^n$ and $x, y \in \mathsf{I\!R}^n$.

A more satisfactory solution, especially when you also need symbols for the natural numbers or rationals, is to use "blackboard" font symbols from the $\mathcal{AMS}$-TeX package (see §5.1 and Appendix E for more information on packages). This requires the command

```
\usepackage{amsfonts}
```

in the preamble. Then `$\mathbb{CNQRZ}$` gives $\mathbb{CNQRZ}$. The command `\mathbb`, like `\mathcal`, provides only uppercase letters and must be used in math mode.

```
A norm $\|\cdot\|: \mathbb{C}^n
\mapsto \mathbb{R}$ is defined
on $\ell_2$ by
\[
  \|\mathbf{x}\| = \left(
      \sum_{j=1}^n |x_j|^2
    \right)^{1/2}.
\]
```

A norm $\| \cdot \| : \mathbb{C}^n \mapsto \mathbb{R}$ is defined on ℓ_2 by
$$\|\mathbf{x}\| = \left(\sum_{j=1}^{n} |x_j|^2 \right)^{1/2}.$$

3.8.4 Binomial Coefficient

The math symbol for the binomial coefficient is defined in the next example using an `array` environment. The commands `@{}` in the column format of `array` suppress the spaces that would normally be placed in those positions (i.e., before and after the first column).

```
\newcommand{\bin}[2]{
   \left(
     \begin{array}{@{}c@{}}
       #1  \\  #2
     \end{array}
   \right)          }
The $n$th Bernstein
polynomial of the function
$f\in C[0,1]$ is defined by
\[
  B_n(x) = \sum_{i=0}^n
    \bin{n}{i}
    f(i/n)
    x^i(1-x)^{n-i},
\]
where
\[
  \bin{n}{i} = \frac{n!}{i!(n-i)!}.
\]
```

The nth Bernstein polynomial of the function $f \in C[0,1]$ is defined by

$$B_n(x) = \sum_{i=0}^{n} \binom{n}{i} f(i/n) x^i (1-x)^{n-i},$$

where

$$\binom{n}{i} = \frac{n!}{i!(n-i)!}.$$

More generally, @{*argument*} replaces the intercolumn space with *argument* (in the previous example the @{} command had an empty argument). This may be used, for example, to construct tables of numbers with the decimal points aligned.

```
Newton's method generates the
sequence $\{x_n\}$ given in the
following Table.
\begin{center}
  \begin{tabular}{c | c r @{.} l}
    $n$ & $x_n$ &
      \multicolumn{2}{c}%
      {Relevant Digits}        \\
    \hline
    0 & 20.0000000 & 20 &      \\
    1 & 10.0500000 & 10 &      \\
    2 &  5.1245025 &  5 &      \\
    3 &  2.7573921 &  2 &      \\
    4 &  1.7413576 &  1 &      \\
    5 &  1.4449434 &  1 & 4    \\
    6 &  1.4145403 &  1 & 414 \\
    7 &  1.4142136 &  1 & 4142136
  \end{tabular}
\end{center}
The third column illustrates the
rapid convergence of the Newton
iteration once the fixed point is
approached.
```

Newton's method generates the sequence $\{x_n\}$ given in the following Table.

n	x_n	Relevant Digits
0	20.0000000	20.
1	10.0500000	10.
2	5.1245025	5.
3	2.7573921	2.
4	1.7413576	1.
5	1.4449434	1.4
6	1.4145403	1.414
7	1.4142136	1.4142136

The third column illustrates the rapid convergence of the Newton iteration once the fixed point is approached.

Chapter 4

Further Essential LATEX

4.1 Document Classes and the Overall Structure

The example on page 6 shows a full LATEX file, which begins with the command

`\documentclass{article}`

This command tells LATEX that the document is to have the **article** class. Other classes that are available include **report, book, slides**, and **letter**. The different classes vary in the range of optional arguments that are available and also in some of the predefined formatting commands. We concentrate in this section on information that applies to the **article** and **report** classes; Appendix D deals with the **slides** class. The **article** class is designed for relatively short documents, such as journal papers, while **report** is meant for longer works that are broken into chapters.

As an alternative to the standard classes built into LATEX, you can use any available class that has been appropriately defined in a file with a **cls** extension. Suppose that the file is called **myclass.cls**. Then the opening command `\documentclass{myclass}` can be used. A description of how to set up a new class is beyond the scope of this book; see [3, 7] if you wish to know more.

If you are preparing a long, specialized document, such as a thesis, then you may benefit from a customized document class. If you are fortunate, your institution will already have a class available, complete with documentation and sample files. Many **cls** files that have been written by other LATEXers are available over the Internet.

It is possible to specify optional arguments to the `\documentclass` command inside square braces. For example, the default type size of 10 points can be enlarged to 11 points (10% bigger) by specifying

`\documentclass[11pt]{article}`

Replacing **11pt** by **12pt** would give a type size of 12 points (20% bigger than the default). Note that 11pt and 12pt are the only available variations on the default size of 10pt.

Another optional argument that we could specify with the **article** class is **twocolumn**, which formats the document with two columns per page. The **a4paper** option expands the page formatting dimensions in a way that is suitable for European A4 paper (8.25 by 10.75 inches). Several optional arguments, separated by commas, can be listed in the square braces, so we could choose

```
\documentclass[12pt,a4paper,twocolumn]{article}
```

4.2 Titles for Documents

A title page can be generated automatically by specifying the title, authors, affiliations, and date. For example, a simplified version of the title page for this book could be generated by the commands

```
\title{Learning \LaTeX}

\author{David F. Griffiths\\
    University of Dundee
    \and
    Desmond J. Higham\\
    Strathclyde University}

\date{June 1996}

\maketitle

\begin{abstract}
  The abstract is optional....
\end{abstract}
```

Learning LATEX

David F. Griffiths
University of Dundee

Desmond J. Higham
Strathclyde University

June 1996

Abstract

The abstract is optional....

The output corresponds to that from \documentclass{article}. Here the \maketitle command tells LATEX to format the title page, using the information supplied by the \title, \author, and \date commands. If there is more than one author, as in the example above, their names are separated by \and. An optional abstract environment is also available, as shown; this is usually placed immediately after the \maketitle command. A further illustration of the use of \maketitle with **article** class is given in Appendix B and with **report** class in Appendix C.

It is possible to add footnotes, for example, to recognize financial support, using the \thanks command. Hence, we could replace David F. Griffiths in this example by

David F. Griffiths\thanks{Supported by the Bearded Welshman Preservation Society.}

A \thanks footnote can be attached to any word appearing inside the \title, \author, or \date. If the \date command is omitted, then the current date is generated; to suppress the date use \date{} with an empty argument.

4.3 Sectioning Commands

We can regard LaTeX documents as organized hierarchically into units such as words, sentences, paragraphs, and sections. The command

\section{Introduction}

creates a section whose heading is Introduction. Each time it encounters the \section command, LaTeX starts a new section. The section heading, such as Introduction, is specified between curly braces and the section number is generated automatically. As for displayed equations, we may give the section a key, for example, intro, by using

\section{Introduction}\label{intro}

We can refer to that section later in the document using the \ref command

It was shown in Section~\ref{intro} that ...

In the preceding example we used the tilde ~ in Section~\ref{intro} as a "hard space". It acts as an "unbreakable space", ensuring that there will be the usual spacing between Section and the number generated by \ref{intro} but a line break will not be allowed between the two.

The commands \subsection and \subsubsection further subdivide the document and work in the same way as \section. There are also the alternative forms

\section*{...}, \subsection*{...}, \subsubsection*{...}

which differ from their unstarred counterparts in that they don't number the sectional units. With the report class, \chapter is also available. This is a higher-level unit than \section; an example is given in Appendix C.

If your document has one appendix or more, then you must insert the

\appendix

command. When it encounters this command, LATEX treats all subsequent sections (with `article` class) or chapters (with `report` class) as appendices and numbers them accordingly; see Appendix C for an example of the latter.

One of LATEX's most simple and powerful commands is `\tableofcontents`. This causes LATEX to produce a table of contents, like the one at the start of this book, based on the the chapter/section/subsection hierarchy in the document. LATEX stores the information that it needs to produce the table of contents in a file with the `toc` extension. Each time you run LATEX on the `tex` file, the information in the `toc` file is updated. (Hence, after a significant change to the `tex` file, it is necessary to run LATEX twice to get the correct table of contents.) The analogous commands `\listoftables` and `\listoffigures` work in the same way, producing files with extensions `lot` and `lof`, respectively.

Returning to `example.tex` on page 6, you will see that the text is contained in the `document` environment. This pattern must always be followed—the main part of the file appears between `\begin{document}` and `\end{document}`. Certain commands, such as `\newcommand` (page 26), are allowed to appear in the preamble, that is, between `\documentclass` and `\begin{document}`. Some commands, such as `\usepackage` (page 45) and `\makeindex` (page 51), must *only* appear in the preamble.

Figure 4.1 shows the typical structure of a document using `article` class. Only the commands `\documentclass`, `\begin{document}`, and `\end{document}` are compulsory. In particular, the commands producing the table of contents and the index (see §5.5) are usually not required for short documents. Also, rather than having the entire document in a single `tex` file, it is often more convenient to develop units such as sections or subsections in separate files and to call them up from a "root" file using the `\input` command; see §5.2.

4.4 Miscellaneous Extras

In this section we describe some miscellaneous details that are worthy of note.

4.4.1 Spacing

LATEX attempts to follow the accepted practice of adding extra space after a period (full stop) that ends a sentence. Any period that immediately follows a lowercase letter and is followed by the blank space character is interpreted by LATEX as marking the end of a sentence. On the occasions where this interpretation is incorrect, it is good practice to override the default. A backslash followed by the space character forces a normal interword space.

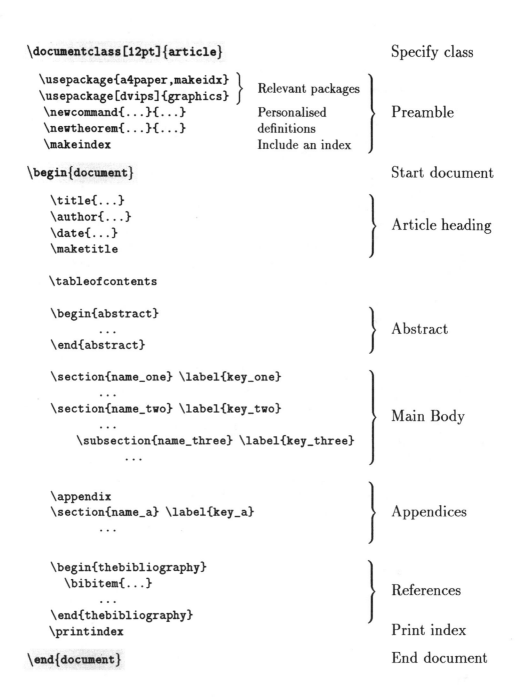

Figure 4.1: The structure of a document with **article** class. Only the highlighted lines are essential.

```
Avoid unnecessary examples,
e.g.\ this one.

Incomplete lists etc.\
are signs of lazy writing.
```

> Avoid unnecessary examples, e.g. this one.
> Incomplete lists etc. are signs of lazy writing.

In a similar vein, to obtain the correct spacing after a sentence that ends with an uppercase letter, the \@ command is needed.

```
Capitalizing for emphasis is
UGLY and DISTRACTING\@.
Another cheap gimmick
is.....................suspense.
```

> Capitalizing for emphasis is UGLY and DISTRACTING. Another cheap gimmick is.......................suspense.

Difficulties with spacing can also arise when commands are used to produce text. For example, the command \LaTeX produces the logo LATEX. Blank spaces after the string \LaTeX have no effect on the output—an interword space must be added where necessary.

```
Many \LaTeX\ users'
punctuate incorrectly;
other \LaTeX ers are more
punctilious.

In your quest for
knowledge about \LaTeX ,
stop at nothing.
```

> Many LATEX users' punctuate incorrectly; other LATEXers are more punctilious.
> In your quest for knowledge about LATEX, stop at nothing.

An interword space was included after \LaTeX on the first line while \LaTeX and ers merged to form "LATEXers" . In the second example, we could use \LaTeX, instead of \LaTeX , (the comma cannot be part of a command name and hence it signals that the command has ended).

4.4.2 Accented Characters

Table 4.1 lists some commands that produce foreign accents and other symbols.

\`{a}	à	\'{e}	é	\"{u}	ü	\H{o}	ő	\.{u}	u̇
\^{o}	ô	\v{c}	č	\u{o}	ŏ	\c{c}	ç	\d{s}	ş
\~{n}	ñ	\t{oo}	o͡o	\={c}	c̄	\b{c}	c̲	\OE	Œ
\AA	Å	\aa	å	\AE	Æ	\ae	æ	\oe	œ
\ss	ß	\O	Ø	\o	ø	\L	Ł	\l	ł
\S	§	\P	¶	?`	¿	!`	¡	\#	#
\dag	†	\ddag	‡	\%	%	\&	&	_	_
\copyright	©	\pounds	£	\$	$	\{	{	\}	}

Table 4.1: Accents and other symbols.

```
We can therefore properly set
the names of the well-known
Scandinavian Numerical Analysts
\AA ke Bj\"orck from Sweden
and S.~P.~N\o rsett from
N\o rway!
```

> We can therefore properly set the names of the well-known Scandinavian Numerical Analysts Åke Björck from Sweden and S. P. Nørsett from Nørway!

Recall from page 35 that each ~ in S.~P.~N\o rsett is an "unbreakable space" that prevents a line break. This ensures that the spacing between the initials and surname will remain but the whole name, initials+surname, will be treated as one word and not be broken across a line boundary.

4.4.3 Dashes and Hyphens

Care must be taken to distinguish between the three types of hyphen that connect words, specify a range, and punctuate; these are produced with -, --, and ---, and give -, –, and —, respectively. (In some circumstances typesetting convention dictates that the -- hyphen should also be used to connect words [4, page 153]). The math minus ($-$ produced by $-$) is yet another type of dash.

```
\begin{enumerate}
\item Introduce meaningless
jargon on a strict
need-to-know basis.

\item Never reveal your sources
(\emph{Alistair Watson},
The Autobiography,
pages 22--23.)

\item Sarcasm---yes, I bet that
will go down really well.
\end{enumerate}
```

1. Introduce meaningless jargon on a strict need-to-know basis.

2. Never reveal your sources (*Alistair Watson*, The Autobiography, pages 22–23.)

3. Sarcasm—yes, I bet that will go down really well.

4.4.4 Quotation Marks

The double quotes character " is rarely used in LaTeX documents. Left and right double quotes should be produced with pairs of single quotation marks.

```
\begin{description}
\item[Wrong:] My old high school
   English teacher put it
   perfectly when she said:
"Quoting is lazy. Express things
   in your own words."
\item[Right:] She also said:
 ''Don't use that trick of
   paraphrasing......[other
   people's words]......inside
   a quote.''
\end{description}
```

Wrong: My old high school English teacher put it perfectly when she said: "Quoting is lazy. Express things in your own words."

Right: She also said: "Don't use that trick of paraphrasing......[other people's words]......inside a quote."

4.5   Troubleshooting

When you run LATEX, processing might come to a premature end with a message that looks like

```
! LaTeX Error: \begin{itemize} on input line 26 ended by \end{document}.

See the LaTeX manual or LaTeX Companion for explanation.
Type  H <return>  for immediate help.
  ...

l.133 \end{document}

?
```

This is an error message—it tells you that LATEX thinks there is a mistake in your file. In this case the environment opened on line 26 of the tex file has not been closed. (If you are processing several files by means of the \input command, then the line number relates to the last file to be used—file names are displayed on the screen as they are included.)

After displaying an error message, the ? signifies that LATEX is waiting for a response from you. Hitting the Return (or Enter) key tells LATEX to continue processing, typing x followed by Return causes LATEX to stop, and typing h followed by Return produces a helpful message about the nature of the error. For the sake of efficiency, it is a good policy to take note of the error messages and hit Return by default—you may need to do this several times. Once the processing is finished, you can make the appropriate edits to the tex file. Sometimes, however, an error has so many consequences that it is necessary to stop the processing with x. A list that includes other responses is given in Table 4.2.

In addition to displaying information on the screen, LATEX produces a log file; this usually has the log extension. The log file contains all the error and warning messages, as well as other information. If there are more than a few

Table 4.2: Your options when LaTeX gives an error message.

Response by you	Action from LaTeX
Return (or Enter)	Continue processing.
?	Type a list of possible actions.
h	Give a slightly more helpful error message.
r	Run without stopping; subsequent error messages are reported but no further action is required from the user. This is likely to generate substantial output from LaTeX.
q	Run quietly; no further error messages will be issued.
x	Stop.
e	Edit file; the default editor is summoned and the cursor placed at the reported location of the error.

errors it may be worthwhile to load the log file into your editor to inspect its contents more closely.

4.5.1 Pinpointing the Error

Although information is provided by the error message and the help facility, there are occasions when an error is difficult to track down. There are several techniques for pinpointing an error.

- If a dvi file has been produced, then preview or print the output. This may make the error apparent.

- Insert the \end{document} command before the line on which the error was detected and run LaTeX on this abbreviated document to check that it is processed without error.

  Now move \end{document} a little further down the document and run LaTeX again. Repeat this procedure until the error is reported. This allows you to narrow down the suspect text.

- Copy the file to junk.tex. Repeatedly delete text from junk.tex and run LaTeX until you have the smallest possible file that reproduces the error. By this point the error should be apparent.

4.5.2 Common Errors

Among the most common errors are

- Unsymmetric delimiters, for example, a { without a matching }, a \begin without the corresponding \end or in-line mathematics without a matching pair of $s. These produce error messages of the type

```
! Paragraph ended before \ref was complete.
<to be read again>
                        \par
1.51
?
```

caused by \ref{key (no closing brace), or

```
! Missing $ inserted.
<inserted text>
                $
1.56
?
```

caused by nonmatching $s.

- Mistyped commands, for example, \begin{centre} rather than \begin{center}.

- Mathematical commands, such as \sin or x_n, in a nonmathematical environment.

- A blank line in an equation environment.

- A missing space or other delimiter after a command. For example, typing \sinx rather than \sin x will cause an error since the command \sinx is not recognized.

- An "ordinary" occurrence of one of the special characters (%, $, #, etc.) without a preceding \ (see page 7).

- Double subscripts or superscripts, for example, the ambiguous x_n_i rather than ${x_n}_i$, which produces x_{ni}, or x_{n_i}, which produces x_{n_i}.

If LATEX stops processing with a *, this may be due to a missing \end{document}; you should respond with \stop.

   In order to make it easier to deal with errors, it is good practice to run LATEX on various intermediate versions of a document as it builds up. In this way you should avoid having a large number of errors that propagate through the document. Alternatively, by exploiting the \input command (see §5.2), you can run LATEX on different parts of the document before putting it all together.

4.5.3 Warning Messages

Messages that begin with the ! sign denote errors. These have to be fixed before the entire document can be properly processed. LATEX also produces warning messages, such as

```
Overfull \hbox (3.07341pt too wide) in paragraph at lines 342--342
```

In this case the warning relates to an overfull \hbox—a good place to break line 342 (of the tex file) could not be found and so the output will extend beyond the right margin; an instance of this has been deliberately included below. Warnings such as these are probably best ignored until the "final" version of the document is ready, after which it may be necessary to insert \linebreak or \pagebreak commands, which force line breaks and page breaks, respectively.

Some common warning messages related to labeling and cross-referencing are exemplified by

LaTeX Warning: Label 'eq:pde' multiply defined.
> Using the key eq:pde more than once in the same document.

LaTeX Warning: Citation 'Lampurt' on page 3 undefined on input line 184.
> A bibliography entry corresponding to the key in a \cite was not found. You may have mistyped the key or forgotten to include the entry in thebibliography (see §5.4).

LaTeX Warning: Reference 'eqn' on page 3 undefined on input line 178.
> The key eqn in a \ref was not found. You may have mistyped the key or forgotten to include a definition using \label (see page 12).

LaTeX Warning: There were undefined references.

LaTeX Warning: There were multiply-defined labels.
> These are both printed at the conclusion of processing in case you missed the earlier warnings.

LaTeX Warning: Label(s) may have changed.

Rerun to get cross-references right.
> This warning appears when you add to or alter the information that determines cross-references for equations, tables, sections, etc. LATEX handles cross-referencing with a two-pass algorithm; consequently you must run LATEX twice (sometimes three times) in order for information to be updated. (If you omit the extra run, then you face the possibility of incorrect cross-references.)

If, even after following the tips above, you have trouble locating an error or understanding a message, then the information in Chapter 8 of [6] may prove useful.

Chapter 5

More About LaTeX

5.1 Packages

The basic capabilities of LaTeX can be greatly enhanced by the use of *packages*. A package, which takes the form of a file with a `sty` extension, can be used to alter formatting parameters, create new environments, and define (or redefine) commands. Many packages are available, covering tasks such as producing special boxes, formatting computer programs, and generating obscure mathematical symbols, in addition to adding extra features to commands like `\verbatim` and `\cite`. The book [3] gives a comprehensive description of over one hundred packages, all of which can be obtained over the Internet (see Appendix E).

If you are working in a multiuser environment, some of the more common packages are probably available to you automatically. A list of packages that come with the standard distribution of LaTeX can be found in [7]; details on how to aquire this file, along with other documentation for packages, are given in Appendix E.

It is possible to write your own packages; however, whatever your requirements, it is likely that something suitable already exists.

The packages `amsfonts` (page 31), `graphics` (page 46), and `makeidx` (page 51) are mentioned elsewhere in this book. The command `\usepackage`, which may appear only in the preamble, tells LaTeX to load a package. Options are included in square braces.

5.2 Inputting Files

It is often natural and convenient to prepare a document as a collection of separate files. This can be done by creating a "root" file, say `main.tex`, in which the `\input` command is used. Suppose `main.tex` contains the command `\input{section1}`. Then when LaTeX is run on `main.tex`, the output produced (in `main.dvi`) is identical to that which would have been produced if `\input{section1}` had been replaced by the contents of the file `section1.tex`. In other words, LATEX reads in the file at the appropriate point.

This facility is useful for several reasons. First, it lets you work with relatively small files, which are easier to edit. Second, it allows you to speed up the debugging phase by selectively including certain parts of a large document. Third, it gives you the chance to set up a collection of frequently arising `\newcommand` declarations (see §3.6) that can be read into to all your documents. Note, however, that when submitting an article for publication, you may be required to provide a single `tex` file.

5.3 Inputting Pictures

You may wish to display pictures, such as function plots or digitized photographs, that have been generated by some other computer package. This can usually be done with the `\includegraphics` command. In this book we focus on graphical files that are stored in PostScript (or encapsulated PostScript) form, and we assume that the `dvips` program is to be used to convert from `dvi` to PostScript. In this case, the `graphics` package must be loaded with the `dvips` option; that is,

`\usepackage[dvips]{graphics}`

must appear in the preamble. (See §5.1 for more information about packages.) The command `\includegraphics{pic.eps}` will cause the picture contained in `pic.eps` to appear in the document.

By making `\includegraphics{pic.eps}` the second argument of the command `\scalebox{...}{...}`, the size of the picture may be scaled by a factor specified by its first argument; an example is given on the next page.

It is common to present a picture as a figure, so that it can be captioned, labeled, and referenced. This can be done with the `figure` environment, which creates a floating body in the same way as the `table` environment discussed on page 13. The following LATEX commands produce Figure 5.1 on the next page.

```
\begin{figure}[hp]
   \begin{center}
      \scalebox{0.3}{\includegraphics{pic.eps}}
   \end{center}
  \caption{An included picture.}
  \label{myfig}
\end{figure}
```

Other graphics formats can be accommodated if you have the appropriate "drivers" on your system. Your local guide should tell you what is available. Optional arguments to `\includegraphics` make it possible to clip the picture,

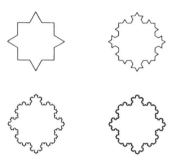

Figure 5.1: An included picture.

while \rotatebox{...}{...} allows it to be rotated (the first argument is the amount of rotation in degrees, and the second is the \includegraphics command). Details can be found in [2, 3, 6, 9].

5.4 Making a Bibliography

A bibliography can be created with the **thebibliography** environment. This is similar to the list-making environments discussed in §2.3.1. The command \bibitem, whose argument is enclosed in curly braces, precedes each entry. The argument specifies the key by which the entry can be cited, anywhere in the document, using the \cite command.

Example 1 The example on the next page shows that more than one key can be given to the \cite command. Multiple keys must be separated by commas (but not by spaces). The example also illustrates the use of the optional extra argument for \cite. If text is enclosed in square braces before the main argument (which is enclosed in curly braces), then this text is added to the citation. Note the second argument "{99}" in

\begin{thebibliography}{99}

This is required to give LATEX an upper limit on the width of the labels appearing in the bibliography list. In our example the labels are 1, 2, 3, and 4, none of which are wider than "99". If the number of entries was between 100 and 999 then we would use \begin{thebibliography}{999}.

Example 2 Our second example shows that it is possible to override the numerical labeling, 1, 2, ..., by including the optional extra argument of \bibitem. This optional argument is enclosed in square braces before the main argument and is used by LATEX for the label.

Additional examples are given in Appendices B and C. This approach of constructing a **thebibliography** environment is fine for bibliographies you will use only once. However, if it is likely that over the course of a few years you will write several LaTeX documents with similar bibliographies, then we strongly recommend the BibTeX program described in [3, 6, 8].

```
The \textttt{thebibliography}
environment appears below.
We can refer to items by their
keys. For example, I have read
\cite{Bryson,Schwartz}
and I am currently reading
\cite[page~134]{Leunen}.
Most of the words in
\cite{Bryson,Leunen,Schwartz}
can be found, in a different
order, in \cite{OED}.

\begin{thebibliography}{99}

\bibitem{Bryson}
  Bill Bryson,
  \emph{The Penguin Dictionary
  of Troublesome Words},
  second ed., Penguin, London,
  1987. ISBN 0-14-051200-4.

\bibitem{Leunen}
  Marie-Claire van Leunen,
  \emph{A Handbook for Scholars},
  revised ed., Oxford University
  Press, New York, 1992.
  ISBN 0-19-506954-4.
  First edition Knopf, 1978.

\bibitem{OED}
  Oxford University Press,
  \emph{The Oxford English
  Dictionary}, second ed., 1989.

\bibitem{Schwartz}
  David Louis Schwartz,
  \emph{How to be a published
  mathematician without trying
  harder than necessary}, in
  The Journal of Irreproducible
  Results: Selected Papers,
  third ed., George H. Scherr,
  ed., 1986, p.~205.

\end{thebibliography}
```

The `thebibliography` environment appears below. We can refer to items by their keys. For example, I have read [1, 4] and I am currently reading [2, page 134]. Most of the words in [1, 2, 4] can be found, in a different order, in [3].

Bibliography

[1] Bill Bryson, *The Penguin Dictionary of Troublesome Words*, second ed., Penguin, London, 1987. ISBN 0-14-051200-4.

[2] Marie-Claire van Leunen, *A Handbook for Scholars*, revised ed., Oxford University Press, New York, 1992. ISBN 0-19-506954-4. First edition Knopf, 1978.

[3] Oxford University Press, *The Oxford English Dictionary*, second ed., 1989.

[4] David Louis Schwartz, *How to be a published mathematician without trying harder than necessary*, in The Journal of Irreproducible Results: Selected Papers, third ed., George H. Scherr, ed., 1986, p. 205.

In this bibliography, we have specified nonnumeric labels for the references. If we had the power to award prizes for the most appropriate coauthor names, or author/title combination, then we would confer runners-up badges to \cite{BC} and \cite{GB}, and first prize to \cite{ABG}. A participation pin acknowledging outstanding effort would go to \cite{Co}.

```
\begin{thebibliography}{Alpher48}

\bibitem[Alpher48]{ABG}
  Alpher, R.A., Bethe, H. and
  Gamow, G.,
  \emph{The origin of chemical
  elements},
  Physical Review,
  \textbf{73}, 1948,
  803--804.

\bibitem[Box64]{BC}
  Box, G. E. P. and Cox, D. R.
  \emph{An analyisis of
  transformations (with
  discussion)},
  J. Royal Stat. Soc.,
  Series B, \textbf{26},
  1964, 211--246.

\bibitem[Green80]{GB}
  Green, H. C. and Brown, R. A.,
  \emph{The acceptability of risk},
  Science and Public Policy,
  \textbf{7}, 1980, 307--318.

\bibitem[Cock63]{Co}
  Cock, A. G.,
  \emph{Genetical studies on
  growth and form in the fowl},
  Genet. Res. Camb.,
  \textbf{4}, 1963, 167--192.

\end{thebibliography}
```

In this bibliography, we have specified nonnumeric labels for the references. If we had the power to award prizes for the most appropriate coauthor names, or author/title combination, then we would confer runners-up badges to [Box64] and [Green80], and first prize to [Alpher48]. A participation pin acknowledging outstanding effort would go to [Cock63].

Bibliography

[Alpher48] Alpher, R.A., Bethe, H. and Gamow, G., *The origin of chemical elements*, Physical Review, **73**, 1948, 803–804.

[Box64] Box, G. E. P. and Cox, D. R. *An analyisis of transformations (with discussion)*, J. Royal Stat. Soc., Series B, **26**, 1964, 211–246.

[Green80] Green, H. C. and Brown, R. A., *The acceptability of risk*, Science and Public Policy, **7**, 1980, 307–318.

[Cock63] Cock, A. G., *Genetical studies on growth and form in the fowl*, Genet. Res. Camb., **4**, 1963, 167–192.

5.5   Making an Index

If you wish to make an index, like the one at the back of this book, LATEX
offers some helpful facilities. We assume here that you will use the program
MakeIndex, which is available over the Internet (see Appendix E).   This
program removes a lot of the tedium from index creation.

We shall give a number of examples, many of which are taken from different
parts of this book. We recommend that you refer to the index in each case to
see the effect.

The first step in generating an entry in the index is to insert the `\index`
command in the relevant location. For example, the entry for "comments" in
the index at the back of this book refers to page 7 and the LATEX source to
generate that part of the page looks like

```
...a mechanism for inserting comments\index{comments} into...
```

The `\index` command has no effect on the text appearing on page 7. However,
it causes LATEX to make a note of the page number, which can then be used
for the index entry. To make sure that the correct page number appears in
the index we leave no space between the word `comments` and the command
`\index{comments}`. (Otherwise, if "comments" happened to be the last word
on the page then the `\index` command would relate to the next page.)

It is important not to add leading spaces inside the index command. If we
had used `\index{ comments}` instead of `\index{comments}` then the entry
would have appeared at the start of the index, since LATEX deems that the
leading space comes before "a" in the alphabet.

The `%` character described on page 7 is useful if you want to make your
indexing commands stand out in the LATEX file. In the example above we could
have used

```
   ...a mechanism for inserting
     \index{comments}%
   comments into...
```

Here, since LATEX ignores everything that follows `%` on the same line (plus
any leading spaces on the next line), there is effectively no space between
`\index{comments}` and `comments`.

Subentries can also be created. On page 38 we have used

```
...produce foreign accents\index{accents!foreign} and other...
```

to get the corresponding index entry. The ! character starts a new level. Up
to three levels are possible, as in

```
Up to three levels%
\index{index!subentry!level-three}
are possible, as in ...
```

It is possible to have multiple entries, as we did on page 23 with

```
The
\index{braces!curly}%
\index{curly braces}%
curly braces
```

We may specify a command of the form \index{*string1*@*string2*}. In this case, *string1* determines the alphabetic position in the index, but *string2* is used as the entry. This is an extremely useful feature. For example, our index contains entries that were produced by[1]

```
\index{bigskip@\verb+\bigskip+}
\index{eqnarray@\texttt{eqnarray} environment}
```

Cross-referencing within the index is easily achieved. To refer the reader from *entry1* to *entry2*, use the command \index{*entry1*|see{*entry2*}}. For example, we used

```
\index{full stop|see{period}}
```

in forming our index. The | character can also be used to specify a range of pages: use \index{*entry*|(} at the start of the range and \index{*entry*|)} at the end. We used \index{index|(} and \index{index|)} at the beginning and end of this section, respectively.

In order for your \index commands to produce the desired effect you must include the package makeidx; this can be done by putting the command

```
\usepackage{makeidx}
```

in the preamble. The command

```
\makeindex
```

must also be included in the preamble. Finally, put the command

```
\printindex
```

where the index is to appear—usually immediately before \end{document}. Figure 4.1 shows a typical set-up involving these commands.

Once you have included the appropriate commands in your document, the index is generated in the following manner. Suppose the LATEX file is called filename.tex. Then the first step is to run LATEX on this file, in the usual way. In addition to the other files with extensions dvi, aux, log, etc., LATEX will create filename.idx. (If you inspect this file, you will see that it contains the entry/pagenumber information that defines the index.) Next, run the program *MakeIndex* on filename.idx; the syntax for this will depend on your computer system, but it is likely to be

---

[1]Note that we used the character + rather than " to make the delimiters for \verb. This is because " has a special meaning as part of an advanced feature of \index. See [3] or [6] for details.

`makeindex filename`

MakeIndex creates the file `filename.ind`. Finally, run LATEX once more on `filename.tex`. The dvi file will now include your index.

In summary, after embedding the correct commands in your document, automatic index generation is a three-stage process: LATEX, *MakeIndex*, and then LATEX again. If you make any changes to the `tex` file that will affect the index, then you must repeat the three stages in order to see the new index.

5.6 Great Moments in LATEX History

1986: First recorded use of the phrase "typographically challenged" in reference to non-LATEX users.

1987: Student writes Ph.D. thesis completely in `verbatim` environment.

1988: Leading mathematical journal rejects manuscript on the grounds that "too many of the variables have fancy tildes over them."

1989: Typing ... instead of `\ldots` becomes a criminal offence.

1989: Number of rainforests that could have been saved if people had bothered to make full use of LATEX previewers reaches double figures.

1990: Killer strain of LATEX evolves, replacing the "`Rerun to get cross-references right`" message with "`Do that again and I delete your files.`"

1991: Bullet overuse receives the official status of "syndrome."

1992: Somebody finally finds a use for the ⋈ symbol.

1992: Extensive testing shows that 98.3% of the time no matter which of the `[h]`, `[t]`, `[b]`, or `[p]` options is used, LATEX will put your `table` at the end of the document.

1993: "`I \heartsuit\␣\LaTeX`" car stickers go on sale.

1994: Latest release of LATEX includes the `\jargonfill` command, which fills the remainder of a page with impressive sounding technical phrases.

1995: Overzealous author publishes book in which every word appears in index.

1995: Positive identification of one thousandth instance of the joke `\index{recursion|see{recursion}}`.

1996: Survey reveals that 6 out of 10 LATEX users think `\iota` will produce an extremely small space and 7 out of 10 LATEX users think that `\ominus` will make something bad happen.

Appendix A

Old LaTeX versus LaTeX 2_ε

This book is aimed at beginners to LaTeX, and it describes the current version, LaTeX 2_ε, which was first released in June 1994. However, it is possible that readers may wish to know something about the differences between LaTeX 2_ε and the earlier version, LaTeX 2.09. (For example, you may be given a draft document in LaTeX 2.09 format by an unenlightened coauthor.) The reference [7] and Appendix D of [6] are excellent sources of information in this area. Here, for completeness, we give a very brief overview of some key differences.

Documents written for LaTeX 2.09 start with the \documentstyle command, whose main argument specifies a document style, as in

\documentstyle{article}

In addition, optional arguments may be supplied in square braces before the main argument. These options correspond to *style files*, with the extension sty, that control the formatting in some way. There are built-in options such as 12pt (for increasing the font size by 20%) and twocolumn (for producing two columns per page). Also, it is possible to use other customized style files. For example,

\documentstyle[12pt,twocolumn,a_style,b_style]{article}

tells LaTeX 2.09 to make use of the built-in 12pt and twocolumn options, along with the style files a_style.sty and b_style.sty.

By contrast, LaTeX 2_ε documents must start with the \documentclass command, as in

\documentclass{article}

Like LaTeX 2.09's \documentstyle, the \documentclass command also allows built-in formatting options such as 12pt and twocolumn to be specified in square braces before the main argument. However, LaTeX 2_ε distinguishes between *options* that can be supplied to \documentclass and *packages*, which must be loaded with \usepackage. (Packages, like LaTeX 2.09's style files, take the form of files with the sty extension.) The LaTeX 2.09 example at the end of the previous paragraph translates to

```
\documentclass[12pt,twocolumn]{article}
\usepackage{a_style,b_style}
```

in LATEX 2_ε. This translation is not guaranteed to work—most, but not all, of the style files written for LATEX 2.09 can be used as packages in LATEX 2_ε. However, even if LATEX 2_ε were to object to `a_style.sty` or `b_style.sty`, it is extremely likely that suitable LATEX 2_ε packages could be found.

LATEX 2_ε contains a number of features that are not available in LATEX 2.09. Examples are the `\ensuremath` command (page 27), the ! option with floating bodies (page 13), and the shape/series/family changing commands for fonts (page 8). It is also worth noting that LATEX 2_ε has better error checking capabilities than LATEX 2.09.

If LATEX 2_ε is run on a LATEX 2.09 document, on seeing the tell-tale `\documentstyle` command the program goes into *compatibility mode* and emulates the older version of LATEX. However, there are two important points to note about compatibility mode:

- it runs more slowly than LATEX 2.09;

- it does not support new LATEX 2_ε features.

Hence, if you are making major changes to a document that is written for LATEX 2.09, we recommend that you begin by converting it to LATEX 2_ε.

Appendix B

A Sample Article

On the next two pages we display the source code and the output of a short article that uses \maketitle, \section, and \includegraphics. We also use \paragraph, which is a convenient means of giving a title to a portion of text, and \today, which generates the current date.

The page number could have been suppressed by placing the command

```
\pagestyle{empty}
```

in the preamble.

The graphical image in the figure has been centered with the command \centering, which differs from the center environment used on page 46 in that it introduces less vertical space.

The addresses of the authors could have been included in the title page by amending the argument of the \author command to

```
\author{S. Kimo\\
        McGills University\\
        Canada
           \and
        R. Poon\\
        University of Whales\\
        U.K.}
```

The source code is available from the Internet site mentioned on page 71.

```
\documentclass{article}
\usepackage[dvips]{graphics}
\begin{document}
  \title{Polar Fishing}
  \author{S. Kimo \and R. Poon}
  \date{Version 3.2: \today}
  \maketitle
\section{Introduction}\label{sec:int}

A \emph{folium} is a generic term for a leaf--shaped curve.  According
to Lawrence~\cite[page 151]{Law}, the curve defined implicitly by the
equation
\begin{equation}\label{eq:f}
  \left(x^2+y^2\right)\left(y^2 + x(x+b)\right) = 4axy^2
\end{equation}
was known to Kepler in 1609 and generates a Simple--, Double-- or
Tri--Folium, when $b\ge 4a$, $b=0$ or $0<b<4a$, respectively.

\subsection{Reparameterization}

To draw the folium defined by equation (\ref{eq:f}) in
Section~\ref{sec:int} it is convenient to change to polar coordinates
$x = r(\theta)\cos\theta$ and $y = r(\theta)\sin\theta$. This leads to
\[
  r(\theta) = -b\cos\theta + 4a\cos\theta\sin^2\theta,
\]
for $0 \le \theta <2\pi$ and is illustrated in Figure~\ref{figa} for
$a=1$, $b=2$.

\begin{figure}[!hp]
  \centering
    \scalebox{.4}{\includegraphics{Folium.eps}}
  \caption{The Tri--folium for $a=1$, $b=2$.}
  \label{figa}
\end{figure}

\paragraph{Acknowledgements}
The definition of the folium was taken from the World Wide Web page
titled ``Famous Curves Index'' that may be found at the address

\verb+http://www-groups.dcs.st-and.ac.uk/~history/Curves/Curves.html+

\noindent  It contains pictures of this and many other curves.
\begin{thebibliography}{9}
  \bibitem{Law} J.~D.~Lawrence, \emph{A Catalog of Special Plane
                        Curves}, Dover Publications, New York, 1972.
\end{thebibliography}
\end{document}
```

Polar Fishing

S. Kimo   R. Poon

Version 3.2: June 26, 1996

1   Introduction

A *folium* is a generic term for a leaf–shaped curve. According to Lawrence [1, page 151], the curve defined implicitly by the equation

$$\left(x^2 + y^2\right)\left(y^2 + x(x + b)\right) = 4axy^2 \tag{1}$$

was known to Kepler in 1609 and generates a Simple–, Double– or Tri–Folium, when $b \geq 4a, b = 0$ or $0 < b < 4a$, respectively.

1.1   Reparameterization

To draw the folium defined by equation (1) in Section 1 it is convenient to change to polar coordinates $x = r(\theta)\cos\theta$ and $y = r(\theta)\sin\theta$. This leads to

$$r(\theta) = -b\cos\theta + 4a\cos\theta\sin^2\theta,$$

for $0 \leq \theta < 2\pi$ and is illustrated in Figure 1 for $a = 1, b = 2$.

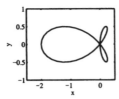

Figure 1: The Tri–folium for $a = 1, b = 2$.

Acknowledgements   The definition of the folium was taken from the World Wide Web page titled "Famous Curves Index" that may be found at the address
      http://www-groups.dcs.st-and.ac.uk/~history/Curves/Curves.html
It contains pictures of this and many other curves.

References

[1] J. D. Lawrence, *A Catalog of Special Plane Curves*, Dover Publications, New York, 1972.

Appendix C

A Sample Report

On the next page the source code is displayed for a short document written using \documentclass{report}. The text is similar to that in Appendix B (where it was formatted in \documentclass{article}), but we have changed occurrences of \section to \chapter and \subsection to \section.

The output shown on page 63 (which we have shrunk to display on a single page) should be compared with that on page 59. You should notice that

- the title, authors, and date (made with \maketitle) now occupy a page of their own, which is unnumbered,

- the layout of the chapter number and title differs from that for section numbers and title in the article class,

- the equations and figures are numbered in the form (a.b) to signify the bth equation (figure) of chapter a,

- the \appendix command causes the subsequent \chapter to produce the chapter heading "Appendix A"; the equation is numbered (A.1).

- the references are now regarded as constituting a separate, unnumbered chapter (called Bibliography) and, because of this, start on a new page.

The source code is available from the Internet site mentioned on page 71.

```
\documentclass{report}
\usepackage[dvips]{graphics}
\begin{document}
  \title{Polar Fishing}
  \author{S. Kimo \and R. Poon}
  \date{Version 3.2: \today}
  \maketitle
\chapter{Introduction}\label{ch:int}

A \emph{folium} is a generic term for a leaf--shaped curve.  According
to Lawrence~\cite[page 151]{Law}, the curve defined by the equation
\begin{equation}\label{eq:f}
  \left(x^2+y^2\right)\left(y^2 + x(x+b)\right) = 4axy^2
\end{equation}
was known to Kepler in 1609 and generates a Simple--, Double-- or
Tri--Folium, when $b \ge 4a$, $b = 0$ or $0 < b < 4a$, respectively.
\section{Reparameterization}
To draw the folium defined by equation (\ref{eq:f}) in
Chapter~\ref{ch:int} it is convenient to change to polar coordinates
$x = r(\theta)\cos\theta$ and $y = r(\theta)\sin\theta$.  This leads to
\begin{equation}
  r(\theta) = -b\cos\theta + 4a\cos\theta\sin^2\theta,
\end{equation}
for $0 \le \theta <2\pi$ and is illustrated on the left of
Figure~\ref{fig:f} for the values $a=1$, $b=2$.
\begin{figure}[!bp]
  \centering
  \scalebox{.35}{\includegraphics{Folium2.eps}}
  \caption{Left: The Tri--folium for $a=1$, $b=2$, Right: a related curve.}
  \label{fig:f}
\end{figure}
\appendix
\chapter{A Related Curve}
A curve of a similar Tri--folium shape is defined~\cite[page 168]{Wie}
by the equation
\begin{equation}
x^4+y^4 + x(x^2-y^2)=0
\end{equation}
and is shown on the right of Figure~\ref{fig:f}.
\begin{thebibliography}{9}
  \bibitem{Law} J.~D.~Lawrence, \emph{A Catalog of Special Plane
            Curves}, Dover Publications, New York, 1972.
  \bibitem{Wie} Heinrich Wieleitner, \emph{Theorie der ebenen
            algebraischen Kurven h\"{o}herer Ordnung},
            G.~J.~G\"{o}schensche Verlangshandlung, Leipzig, 1905.
\end{thebibliography}

\end{document}
```

Polar Fishing

S. Kimo   R. Poon

Version 3.2: June 4, 1996

Chapter 1

Introduction

A *folium* is a generic term for a leaf–shaped curve. According to Lawrence [1, page 151], the curve defined implicitly by the equation

$$\left(x^2 + y^2\right)\left(y^2 + x(x+b)\right) = 4axy^2 \tag{1.1}$$

was known to Kepler in 1609 and generates a Simple–, Double– or Tri–Folium, according to whether $b \geq 4a, b = 0$ or $0 < b < 4a$, respectively.

1.1 Reparameterization

To draw the folium defined by equation (1.1) in Chapter 1 it is convenient to change to polar coordinates $x = r(\theta)\cos\theta$ and $y = r(\theta)\sin\theta$. This leads to

$$r(\theta) = -b\cos\theta + 4a\cos\theta\sin^2\theta, \tag{1.2}$$

for $0 \leq \theta < 2\pi$ and is illustrated on the left of Figure 1.1 for the values $a = 1, b = 2$.

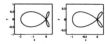

Figure 1.1: Left: The Tri–folium for $a = 1, b = 2$, Right: a related curve.

1

Appendix A

A Related Curve

A curve of a similar Tri–folium shape is defined [2, page 168] by the equation

$$x^4 + y^4 + x(x^2 - y^2) = 0 \tag{A.1}$$

and is shown on the right of Figure 1.1.

2

Bibliography

[1] J. D. Lawrence, *A Catalog of Special Plane Curves*, Dover Publications, New York, 1972.

[2] Heinrich Wieleitner, *Theorie der ebenen algebraischen Kurven höherer Ordnung*, G. J. Göschensche Verlangshandlung, Leipzig, 1905.

3

Appendix D

Slides

The **slides** document class is specially designed for use in the preparation of slides (for display on overhead projectors). After specifying

`\documentclass{slides}`

you must enclose each slide in `\begin{slide}` ... `\end{slide}`. LaTeX will start each slide on a separate page. The output will appear in special large, clear fonts for which only a subset of the usual shape/series/family changing commands (page 8) is available. The default (roman) font has sans serif style, and a typewriter style can also be chosen. Upright and italic shapes can be used, as well as `\emph`.

Because each slide is self-contained, some commands, such as those for creating sections and subsections or page breaking, are not allowed.

A few other points are worthy of note. LaTeX is not a WYSIWYG (What You See Is What You Get) system and hence is not ideally suited to slide preparation. However, if you wish to prepare slides based on mathematical material that is already contained in a LaTeX document, then the relative ease of "importing" the relevant source code into a **slides** document may outweigh the inconvenience of polishing the output by trial and error. Also, although it is recognized as good practice to limit the amount of material on a slide, many people find the content-per-page constraint in **slides** a little unforgiving, especially for mathematical expressions. For this reason, some LaTeX users have "rolled their own" alternative packages for preparing slides in LaTeX.

The following example document illustrates the basic use of the **slides** document class. In Chapter 5 of [6] you can learn about some advanced features for producing overlays and adding information that will help you remember what to say during a presentation and keep track of time.

The source code is available from the Internet site mentioned on page 71.

```
\documentclass{slides}
\usepackage[dvips]{graphics}
\usepackage{color}
\begin{document}

\definecolor{grey}{gray}{.95}
\renewcommand{\fboxrule}{2pt}
%  \stitle is our customized command for
%  producing shaded headings.
\newcommand{\stitle}[1]{
      \begin{center}
         \fbox{\colorbox{grey}{\textbf{\large #1}}}
      \end{center}
                              }
\begin{slide}
  \stitle{Research Skills: Verbal}
  \begin{itemize}
    \item Injecting enthusiasm probably won't do any harm.
    \item Appropriate metaphors are worth their weight in gold.
    \item Before using a clich\'e, run it up the flagpole
          and see if anybody salutes.
    \item There is no place for overemphasis, whatsoever.
    \item Finish your point on an up-beat note, unless you
          can't think of one.
  \end{itemize}
\end{slide}
%          ....... source for slides 2 and 3 deleted .......
\begin{slide}
  \stitle{Research Skills: Evaluation}
  \[
    \mathrm{Impressiveness} =  F^2 C_e \log(C_n)
        \int_0^T X(t)^2 G(t) \, dt,
  \]
  where
  \begin{itemize}
    \item $F$:  total funding,
    \item $C_e$:  \# experimental constants,
    \item $C_n$:  \# numerically computed constants,
    \item $X(t)$:  \# research students at time $t$,
    \item $G(t)$: \texttt{Gigaflop} rate at time $t$.
  \end{itemize}
\end{slide}

\end{document}
```

Research Skills: Verbal

- Injecting enthusiasm probably won't do any harm.

- Appropriate metaphors are worth their weight in gold.

- Before using a cliché, run it up the flagpole and see if anybody salutes.

- There is no place for overemphasis, what-soever.

- Finish your point on an up-beat note, un-less you can't think of one.

1

Research Skills: Written

a) Many readers assume that a word will not assume two meanings in the same sentence.

b) If you can't afford a book on grammar, at least find someone to lend one off.

c) It has been suggested that some words are absolute, not relative. This is very true.

d) In terms of writing convoluted sentences, don't.

N.B.
A strong ending is the last thing you need.

2

Research Skills: Technical

1. It can be shown that you shouldn't miss out too many details.

2. Some writers introduce a large number, N, of unnecessary symbols.

3. Use mathematical jargon iff it is absolutely necessary.

4. And avoid math symbols unless $\exists$ a good reason.

5. Restrict your hyphen-usage.

6. Learn one new math word every day, and you'll soon find your vocabulary growing exponentially.

3

Research Skills: Evaluation

$$\text{Impressiveness} = F^2 C_e \log(C_n) \int_0^T X(t)^2 G(t)\, dt,$$

where

- F: total funding,

- C_e: # experimental constants,

- C_n: # numerically computed constants,

- $X(t)$: # research students at time t,

- $G(t)$: Gigaflop rate at time t.

4

Appendix E

Internet Resources

The resources available on the Internet fall into the broad categories of documentation, software, and hypertext help. We shall not attempt the impossible task of giving comprehensive listings but will give information that those interested may pursue. Currently, [7] provides the most comprehensive information on available resources and how to aquire and install them.

E.1 Documentation

In this section we describe some documentation that comes in the form of `tex` files (or preprocessed in `dvi` or `ps` formats).

`usrguide.tex`

> *LATEX 2ε for authors* [7]. Contents include listings of available classes, packages, and tools as well as features that distinguish LATEX 2ε from LATEX 2.09.

`grfguide.tex`

> *Packages in the 'graphics' bundle* [2]—a user manual for the packages `color`, `graphics` (§5.3), and the extended graphics package `graphicx`.

`epslatex.ps`

> *Using EPS Graphics in LATEX 2ε Documents* [9]. Discusses inclusion of encapsulated PostScript graphics files (also, TIFF, GIF, JPEG, PICT, and other formats) as well as the `subfigure` and `caption2` packages for manipulating the appearance of figures and their captions.

`amsldoc.tex`

> *AMS-LATEX Version 1.2, User's Guide.* The American Mathematical Society's packages for LATEX 2ε [1].

`babel.dvi`

> *Babel, a multilingual package for use with standard document classes.* Describes the LATEX support available for non-English languages.

btxdoc.tex
> The source of BIBTEX*ing* [8].

natbib.tex
> *Natural Sciences Citations and References.* Describes the **natbib** package for alternative citation formats.

makeindex.tex
> *Makeindex: An Index Processor For LATEX* by Leslie Lamport (1987). This describes the version for LATEX 2.09.

If you have a standard installation of LATEX then it is likely that these files are already available to you. The simplest way of finding out about the **tex** files is by typing a command such as

```
latex usrguide.tex
```

If an error message appears, you will have to consult your local guide or download the appropriate files from one of the CTAN sites (§E.2) or via the WWW (§E.3).

E.2   CTAN

The Comprehensive TEX Archive Network (CTAN) is the primary source of information. It consists of a set of essentially identical Internet sites for software and information relating to LATEX. In particular, the documentation described in the previous section, implementations of LATEX, user-supplied packages, and answers to frequently asked questions are available.

The **ftp** addresses of the three main participating CTAN sites are

ftp.cdrom.com	USA
ftp.dante.de	Germany
ftp.tex.ac.uk	Great Britain

and you should select the server closest to you in order to keep network load to a minimum. There are many other mirrored sites; these are listed in the file **/pub/archive/CTAN.sites** available from any of the above addresses.

E.3   WWW

The "official" home page for LATEX on the World Wide Web (WWW) is accessible from the Uniform Resource Locator (URL)

```
http://www.tex.ac.uk/CTAN/latex/
```

and provides access to the CTAN **ftp** sites. The following locations may also be of interest.

`http://molscat.giss.nasa.gov/LaTeX/`
> Extensive cross linked files produced by Sheldon Green to provide hypertext help for LaTeX as well as other links to LaTeX information such as FAQs (Frequently Asked Questions), May 1995.

`http://www.tug.org/`
> Home page of TeX Users Group. See §E.5.
> Interesting TeX-related URLs, National TeX Users Groups, FAQs, documentation, CTAN interfaces, Publications, Publishers, Packages and programs, Projects, TeX vendors.

`http://www.stsci.edu/ftp/software/tex/ltxcrib/`
> C. D. Biemesderfer's LaTeX 2.09 Crib sheet. A complete but concise list of all LaTeX 2.09 commands.

The URLs mentioned in this appendix plus the source code for the sample document in Appendices B, C, and D are accessible from
`http://www.mcs.dundee.ac.uk:8080/software/index.html`

E.4   Professional Societies

`http://www.aas.org`
> American Astronomical Society (AASTeX).

`http://www.aip.org`
> American Institute of Physics (REVTeX).

`http://www.ams.org`
> American Mathematical Society. AMSTeX resources as well as access to authoring packages related to AMS publications; LaTeX implementations for PCs and Macs. FTP address: `e-math.ams.org`.

`http://www-chel.anglia.ac.uk/~imacrh/index.html`
> Institute of Mathematics and its Applications (U.K.)

`http://www.siam.org`
> SIAM's home page. Information on SIAM's activities as well as access to LaTeX packages related to SIAM publications.

E.5   TUG

The TeX Users Group (TUG), an organization that offers advice and information about TeX-related matters, can be reached at the email address `tug@tug.org`, via the WWW link listed in §E.3, or by writing to

> TeX Users Group
> 1850 Union Street, #1637
> San Francisco, CA 94123
> U.S.A.

There is a nominal fee for membership to the organization but technical information is available from their web page free of charge.

Bibliography

[1] American Mathematical Society, $\mathcal{AMS}$-LaTeX *Version 1.2, User's Guide*. File: `amsldoc.tex` (see Appendix E).

[2] D. P. Carlisle, *Packages in the 'graphics' bundle*, 1995. File: `grfguide.tex` (see Appendix E).

[3] Michel Goossens, Frank Mittelbach, and Alexander Samarin, *The LaTeX Companion*, Addison-Wesley, Reading, MA, 1994. ISBN 0-201-54199-8.

[4] Nicholas J. Higham, *Handbook of Writing for the Mathematical Sciences*, SIAM, Philadelphia, PA, 1993. ISBN 0-89871-314-5.

[5] Donald E. Knuth, *The TeXbook*, Addison-Wesley, Reading, MA, 1986. ISBN 0-201-13448-9.

[6] Leslie Lamport, *LaTeX: A Document Preparation System. User's Guide and Reference Manual*, 2nd edition, Addison-Wesley, Reading, MA, 1994. ISBN 0-201-52983-1.

[7] LaTeX 3 Project Team, *LaTeX 2_ε for authors*, 1994. File: `usrguide.tex` (see Appendix E).

[8] Oren Patashnik, BibTeX*ing*, File: `btxdoc.tex`, 1988 (see Appendix E).

[9] Keith Reckdahl, *Using EPS Graphics in LaTeX 2_ε Documents*, 1996. File: `epslatex.ps` (see Appendix E).

Index